Judy, This is a late
Christmas Gift. It's the
story of our Missions
Pastor from Free Chapel
Church in Gainesville, Ga.
Love & Prayers, John &
Lola

Vision Caster

Hugh B. Sutton

Vision Caster

The story of Hugh B. Skelton

by E. Amelia Billingsley

ISBN: 0-87148-893-0

Reverend Hugh B. Skelton

CONTENTS

From the Author

In the years of writing this book, much has changed. I met Hugh and Louise Skelton when I was fresh out of college and trying to decide my course in life. Of course, I had heard of "the" missionary couple through church circles, but I did not know them. Seven years of living with them or within 100 yards of them changed that. I have personally seen Hugh change from missionary on the field, to administrator, to traveler of the world, to a man respected throughout more countries than most people can name. I have also seen him in such varied modes as parent, upholsterer, decorator, preacher, teacher, counselor, and hospital patient. The latter was seen more often than was pleasant. And in it all, I have seen a man of patience and love. I have never seen him angry, nor critical, nor vengeful. It is not an act of self-discipline. It is the way he is.

I have listened to his stories, dug through his files, and have pressed him with questions. We have worked on things over meals, while traveling, and sitting in his den at night. By genre, it is actually a biography written in first person. I just found that format to be the most effective. For the omissions from this book, I take responsibility. At my insistence, the names in the book have been kept to a minimum. There are so many that figure prominently into this story that including them would have made the story impossibly long. So, I opted for the route to leave out as many specific names as possible. Those of you who read and recognize your place in this book are not forgotten. But, your story lives on and is not complete. It is yet being written.

We worked for years under a different title for the book. But, as the end neared, I sat at a Cuban restaurant in Atlanta with Allen Skelton. He said words that struck me as the true title of the book. "My dad is a Vision Caster." I had not heard the term before, but I knew he was right. Hugh Skelton casts visions to those who come his way. He makes us believe in right, in world brotherhood, in the equality and quality of all people. He inspires us to give of ourselves for the cause of others. His ability, in light of his many physical limitations and disabilities, makes us believe that we too can make a difference in this world. He casts upon us a vision of the regions beyond — those areas we have not yet reached. Regions beyond our present world, beyond our comfort zone, beyond our known abilities. And, he makes us believe that we can reach to the very edge of what we can see.

Should you find error or flaw as you read, forgive me. I wrote from the heart as much as from my mind. It is my grief that the story is not as well told as it was lived.

~~ *E. Amelia Billingsley*

Special thanks: Gene Eisenberg (cover design); Jeanie Cassity, Allen and Vicky Skelton, Dorothy Waters, Shirley Whitworth (editing assistance).

Part I
Cuba

Born in Weakness
Starting the Work
We Will Stay Forever
Between the Battle Lines
Cuba Libre!

1

Born in Weakness

It is in strange times of need that we learn what sort of persons we really are. I am not one of swearing lips or a screamer of pain, but I surely found myself to be a man of sickness, a gritter of teeth, and a crier out in the night. Why the operation was to take place in such a filthy place, I cannot say. The small operating room still showed the results of the last surgery. The black Cuban doctor was almost a stranger to me except for a brief meeting on the previous day when my sickness began. An appendectomy — just a piece of minor surgery. Yes, in the States with antiseptically clean hospitals and carefully prepared equipment. Oh, to be at home again!

The spinal shot had been horrible. No other word fits the experience. But as the doctor began to cut into the flesh, reality hit me. The left side of my body was deadened; the critical right side was not at all painless. They had anesthetized the wrong side! At the doctor's order, the nurse reached for the gas. It had been rejected before surgery as faulty, having a hole in the mask. Now, it was the only thing to do. That hole and the leakage of air into the anesthesia were to lead me to the edge of death. At least, I felt it so.

Surface clean — that's how the mountain clinic struck me. I lay on the narrow cot in agony of pain and nausea. It was not my first bleak little clinic, and surely would not be my last, but that is a later story. There was an extra cot for "company" and the glassless window with night shutters. The three-room clinic of Palma Soriano would keep me for two more days, two miserable days. The night became long and the post operation attacks of nausea more frequent. Surely, I was dying. At times, I felt the spirit begin to ebb from my body. I heard the low sound of prayer. There were two who stood with me, and in the darkest of nights, they prayed. God seems to give women to bear the prayer burden and ability to comfort the spirit of man in times near death. I was given two in those dark hours.

Our dear faithful "Cuban mama", Consuelo, had come from Santiago as soon as she heard of my sickness. Her mulatto features and shoulder length white hair sank into my fuzzy brain. "Hermano. Hermano Skelton." The soft Cuban Spanish penetrated my brain, but no response would come.

And, with the angelic Consuelo, stood Velda. She and Robert had always been true friends. The two women prayed and watched through the night. But even in the pain and darkness, I knew a longing for two women even dearer to me. Louise, the wife committed to the missionary call, was some 1,500 miles away locked into her own struggle with disease and hemorrhaging. We are cousins, you know — only third cousins and not the kind you ever remember seeing as a child. She says she remembers me from my early youth. I think she makes it up to embarrass me. Always, Louise tells the story of my sister Dorothy and I singing in church and how she remembers us. I certainly have no such memory. But, I do recall quite well how I tried to date her in later years, and she seemed so uninterested. And in the lonely agony of those moments, I could recall every detail of our growing love.

4

The decision to marry is not often so profoundly romantic and simple as writers make it seem. There were other girls that I thought might be good wife material. But, when the leading of the Lord to the mission field came, it was clear that Louise was to be my choice. She came to Cuba first before I even committed myself to missionary work. My sister Dorothy and her husband had been Cuban missionaries for some four years when Louise came for her 14 month visit. She knew her destiny immediately and turned all dreams and plans toward the church and Cuba. My commitment to that same trail came later on a two-week "family visit" with my sister.

That first visit to the island sealed my fate. I had another two years to finish at Mercer University, but then it would be back to Cuba for a lifetime of work, or so I thought. But, why should marriage wait another two years? We married with visions of Cuba in our hearts, and Louise stood by me in that last college year even as she has stood with me and been my helping hand in every other endeavor. Yet, now in Palma Soriano, pain and distress reduced her to only a memory. And the kind hand and sincere prayers of Velda Hough were what God had given to fill the void within. For that, I was thankful.

Consuelo Bosch, the woman who became like a mother to us in Cuba, cared for my family as her own. Her short matronly frame was clothed in the best her talented daughters could produce. She sat by my bed for hours. The neatness to be seen in her spotlessly polished home worked its way into the clinic as she constantly straightened and fussed over my surroundings. We had always called her "mama" though she was not at all like my mother. Only in the matter of love did she compare to the mother I had left in the North Georgia mountains.

I was 25 when Louise and I, with our young son Allen, left Gainesville, Georgia, for Cuba. Our plans were to stay for three years on that first venture. Mother was sick. As she waved from the hospital doorway, her weakness almost overcoming her, I knew I would never see her alive again. Her two children were both gone to a foreign land — a land so far away in the minds of Georgia mountain people — while her sickness drew life from her daily. It must have been an unbearable burden. My tears and her tears had flowed without embarrassment. But commitment requires sacrifice and the future of the young cannot be set aside for grief of a loved one. We left mother in her weakness and returned to her funeral six months later. In my physical pain, the picture of her standing in that doorway, waving her feeble good-bye, floated through my mind.

As a minister, I am well aware of our Lord's promise that the forsaking of loved ones shall lead to His provision in abundance (Matt. 19:29). And so, my life has been filled with those who have cared for me as my own family could desire to do. In this time of need, the Lord provided the kindness of Velda Hough in place of my wife. And in place of a mother, He provided this "Cuban mama" who supplied care, love, and a place of rest when times were difficult. Still, my desire was in truth for the wife and mother who were absent.

Lying in that clinic, there was little sleep to be had. My mind wandered back to the mountains of North Georgia where I was raised. In the tiny town of Cornelia, the doctor announced the birth of a stillborn son to Clifford Skelton. "The baby is dead," was the blunt statement. But, being a man of faith and prayer, my father begged the doctor to enter the room one more time to try to find life in the infant. Agonizing moments and then the weakest of breaths came. Part of the desperation work of resuscitation involved switching my lifeless form from hot to cold water rapidly. Perhaps it was a sign of things to come. In and out of hot water has been a way of life for me at times. The frantic plan worked, and my father knew he had the son God had promised to him. I did not know for many years that there was another part to that promise. My father never wavered in the belief that God had given him a son, and that son would preach the Gospel. He was not wrong.

My physical deficit was immediately apparent. The doctor diagnosed heart problems in the infant with little hope of life into adulthood. The enlarged heart was the size of the head of the baby. There was a definite hole in the heart — "ventricular septal defect" technically. Repair of such is not uncommon today, but those were not days of advanced heart surgery. No repairs were possible then. And, as an adult, the repair is considered too dangerous to attempt. So, the only treatment was years of restricted activity and daily medications to relieve stress around the heart.

How many times did I wish to be normal? How often did I sit in frustration because I had no strength to do the things other children did? No ball games. No races and games of tag. Nothing that might stress the body with a heart of weakness. My attention turned to more sedentary things, like training rabbits. The constant flow of pets took my time. A long line of dogs dotted the chronology of my youth. I raised rabbits, even trained one to come downstairs to eat, then go upstairs for water. What genius I had! It's a wonder the circus didn't become my life.

Mother was never a strong person either. The family had to learn to live with her frequent sickness and unbearable bouts with migraine headaches. It was a suffering known to her entire family and inherited in part by my sister and by me. Yet, mother provided the loving atmosphere that made our family a stable one. From her, we learned to endure difficulties, and from our father, we learned to work our way through them. Kindness and caring were a natural part of our lives.

Education was a problem. The doctor advised, "No school. It is beyond his physical endurance."

My father was persistent. "God will take care of him. He needs an education!"

I did quite a bit to prove the doctor's point rather than my father's. To put it mildly, I was not captivated by the higher intellectual processes or my personal need of them. A dedicated student, I was not. There are opportunities one wishes to have a second time. One such wish for me would be a second chance at the foundations of education. A lack of study in the early years was repaired only by long diligent study in later times.

Memories of childhood are always focused by the physical weakness. Days, months, months absent because of illness. A minor playground scuffle becomes near tragedy when a blow misses its target and hits an innocent bystander (me) in the heart. It got everyone's attention — being carried off the playground near death always does that. Nose bleeds interrupted many a day. Blood vessels growing on top of the protective flesh area of the nose rather than beneath it brought me very realistically near death by bleeding quite often. This was a constant plague until the day of my healing of the condition at age 24. Whatever was happening, Hugh had to be careful not to get sick or hurt.

8

What could I do that fit me into the social strata of a growing boy? NOTHING! Then, at age 12, a great adventure hit me. Boy Scouts! It was my challenge — almost an obsession. I could learn those things. I could do those things. I could earn those badges. The goal of my life became the rank of Eagle Scout. My time was no longer mine; it belonged to the Boy Scout manual, to Boy Scout projects, to Boy Scout goals. Scouting became my road to success and survival. And, I did it well! By age 17, I was an Eagle Scout. My record 86 merit badges stood for many years as a Georgia State record. Because of physical limitations, some requirements were beyond me. But, for everyone, an alternative activity was approved by Scouting administration, and I fulfilled them all.

I THOUGHT the goal was rank and merit badges. What I gained was actually life-giving knowledge. The mission work would one day call on the scouting studies for survival and success. How to survive and have comfort in hostile environments, how to do the practical work of preparing camp meals, etc., how to cooperate with nature and permit it to support me rather than battle the elements — all these were essential to my adult work. But, in my youth, it meant that I could do things. I could do some things better than others. Persistence would win the day. Unusual situations need not be frightening. Personal inadequacy was not to be feared. These were and are the profits reaped from the Scouting experience.

The memories take on energy that I do not have. My illness has drained away the normal emotional vitality of youth. How many hospitals have I known other than this clinic in Cuba? They are more than I can number. But, rural North Georgia did provide a bit better medical care than pre-revolutionary Cuba. My high school days were interrupted in sickness—one whole year missed. Yet, with every hardship comes an advantage. At age 15, I needed transportation and was permitted a model-T Ford, a special driver's license, and transfer to a rural high school convenient for my driving. For my final year, I was able to transfer back to Gainesville High School. There, my speaking skills brought me into true social status with my peers. I could not compete in athletics, but I made my mark in drama. At last, I fit in.

There was also some physical strength developing. Much of my youth was spent with my dad in his furniture shop. "Hand me that tack hammer, son. Can you find me a webbing stretcher?" I longed for the strong grip and muscles to use those tools that he worked with such ease. Visually, I learned the trade long before I could handle the labor. But, it did come. By the time of my college summers, I was working in the upholstery shop beside the man I most admired — my father.

College was a foregone conclusion. My father never questioned me about it. And through two years at Emmanual College, I learned the ministry. Missionary work in Cuba was not unlike ministry in the tiny communities of North Georgia. The Bible-based junior college sent ministry teams out to surrounding areas for weekend work. We (Russell West, Durant Driggers, and myself) started in street ministry in Bowman, Georgia. The three of us learned a lot about public speaking the hard way. As with all of life, the good times linger in thought and the tough times fade. From there we progressed all the way to Sunday School teaching and on-the-job preacher training in a small country church known as David's Home. Emmanuel College started me out, and then the summer upholstery work and the college were left behind for

Mercer University. I was ready for the big city (Macon, Georgia), a preaching job, and family life.

CUBA! Where did I learn of Cuba? It must have been on the maps in high school. Surely, I knew some world geography. Dorothy — my sister — she brought that word home. At least, she made it a living word in our household. Graduation from Brenau, marriage to a minister, and a commitment to go to Cuba all seem to crowd into one event. Dorothy was going to Cuba. Better look that up. How far is it? What language do they speak there? I wonder if I will maybe visit her there some day. It was not the first time I had heard of the country, I am sure. But, it was the first time it took root in my heart and became an important word in my life.

We became more familiar with the island through her letters, through her visits home, and through the visitors she and Bill brought from time to time. It was in August of 1951 that I made my first trip to see it for myself. My life's direction changed more than I could have possibly dreamed. In truth, it would influence every major decision afterwards and radically change my future. For one thing, it led me into a life that would wind up in this mountain clinic unsure of whether to live or die.

"Mira. El Americano. Venga. Mira." What? I am becoming a spectacle — the village theater it seems. The empty window is filled with faces. No bodies, just little black and brown faces. The children of Palma Soriano had no timidity about looking in on my plight. Lord, I would wish for some peace. Yet, those are the faces that caught my heart on that first trip.

I don't know what I really expected of Cuba the first time I saw the island. Though Havana is only 90 miles from Key West, Florida, it is some 650 more miles to the bay at the east end of the island where I was to land. Santiago de Cuba is never to be known for its fine airport, at least not the airport I saw on that first arrival. The shock of coming down in a DC-3 on a single airstrip was nothing compared to the horror of that tiny tin shack which some unfortunate family called home that perched within a stone's throw of the runway's end. The cows that grazed near the single smooth lane took no notice of my coming. It was a strange introduction that was quickly set aside as I saw Dorothy and Louise waiting. Two women again looking out for me, one so dear and another about to become the love of my life. But, at age 23, a mountain boy from Georgia had "arrived" and another love affair was developing.

That first view of the island from the airstrip was not a valid view of the paradise of Cuba. Truly luscious beauty covered the Atlantic island. The greenery of the sugar cane areas, the beauty of the Bay of Santiago, and the immediate rise of the land into green hills and mountains deserve a master poet's description. My sister Dorothy had lived in Cuba for several years as a missionary before that two-week visit that sealed my fate to love the island. She and Bill were missionaries. As we climbed the hill at El Cristo toward their two-story wooden home, the massive banana trees and abundance of greenery gave the impression of a picture postcard. None imagined that this land would be scarred, torn, and beaten by war within a few months — none perhaps except a bearded rebel withdrawn to Mexico. As I discovered Cuba's beauty, Fidel was already plotting ways to destroy her land, her wealth, her people.

My introduction to Cuba was just that, an introduction. I saw the people and was stricken by the island's beauty, her hills, her beaches, the palm trees, wild flowers, and tropical fruits filled with unfamiliar tastes. My language capabilities peaked at "¿Cómo está?" and "Adios." Those tanned Latin faces were equally unfamiliar to me. The Cubans were a mixture of black, white, and brown flowing through streets and shops as one. The poor and the rich were easily distinguished. The learned and the illiterate traveled the same streets. And even with my lack of Spanish, they fascinated me.

The cultural shock waves rolled over me at times. That pleasant home of my sister's was a haven for every crawling creature that God ever made, or so it seemed to me. The tropical climate bred in abundance. Tiny ants could not be kept from the bed while tarantulas hid by the door to slip in with any opening. Killing the huge spiders before going to bed became part of the average evening routine. And, bless us lest we forget, there was the mosquito netting and that nightly battle to find the last mosquito under your net before sleeping. Screens were an unknown.

"You must be insane to live in this," was my first though of Dorothy. But she seemed to have adjusted well, even to the cooking on charcoal. How could one find peace in the insanity of deprivation and crawling creatures? I had first-class cultural shock. It would take something special to get me to like the place. But, that "something special" came with my introduction to the people of Cuba. The melting of my heart began even as any iceberg would in that sweltering Cuban heat. It had its unpleasant parts, but the island's overall charm captivated me and a life-time commitment to its people was born. First impressions can be so wrong. The beauty of Cuba had only need of time to reveal itself to me.

2

Starting the Work

===

I was not on a plane trip now. I lay in a mountain clinic drifting from reality to memory. And the waves of sleep were like the roll of an ocean trip — a ferry ride — like so many more — like that first sickening trip as a family. February 8, 1955. The ferry boat pulled out of Key West, Florida. Destination: Havana, Cuba. Of the 125 cars aboard, one belonged to a greenhorn missionary, his wife, and son. Somewhere on board was a noted author on another trip to his adopted Cuba — or was it another time that I talked with Hemingway on the nine-hour sailing? No matter, the trips all run together after a time. But, this first one — I wonder if it was a view of things to come.

The nine-hour trip became a nightmarish storm that engulfed us, almost a sign of the political storms to come in Cuba over the next six years. The rough seas poured in over either side of the ferry as it rolled in the waters. Seasickness broke out everywhere. And I, so often caught in physical weakness, did not pass up the chance to empty my innermost being into the Gulf of Mexico. Such a rough trip, I have never encountered since then. All but one passenger and the crew lay on sofas, hung over railings, and braced themselves in chairs. Never to be forgotten are those hours I spent on top deck, stretched out over a box of life preservers wondering why I ever ever started this trip. Pillows were shoved between cars to keep them from scraping one another.

The landing at Cardenas, just beyond Havana, was a welcome moment. Never was Cuba embraced so thankfully by a boat load of people. From the storms of the sea, there was little intermission. Then, quickly through customs and an immediate drive Santiago. The 600 plus mile trip brought us to an exhausted halt outside the large two-story duplex that was to be "home." Greetings, food, collapse, and sleep. We were home in Cuba — the beginning of six wonderful frightening years.

First thing had to be settling into the house. We began our furniture purchases at Sears, a good familiar name. In those days, American companies and products were abundant. The more American, the better, was the evaluation of goods among the Cubans then. And I must confess, my own feelings were very much in that direction. But even in these furnishings, my market changed from the major stores to more personal sources. A family household sale drew me to many purchases. It was certainly but a beginning of my affection for the "garage sale," auction-type market place. There are those that contend I will be looking for a "bargain sale" when St. Peter greets me at the Gates.

Language lessons were the next crucial item. In my opinion, it is impossible — totally impossible — for any missionary or other outsider to effectively deal with a population without an understanding of the language. The major key to a culture lies in its language and communication. Any effort at lasting change or influence must be based on a respect and understanding of that local culture. This deep conviction led me down a rocky road of study. To Louise, the Spanish language came relatively easy. By the time of our arrival, she already spoke Spanish quite well. Her previous stay in Cuba for 14 months left her

16

very capable of extended conversation. For me, it would take many many hours of study. Three classes of college Spanish in the U.S. had brought three "D's". My first year in Cuba required some five hours a day of language study. I had private tutors from the nearby university. My first sermons were read from carefully written and corrected pages of Spanish. Fluent Spanish for me was not a gift, it was the product of grinding labor, frustration, and practice, practice, practice.

Starting language classes was a fairly simple thing; starting a church work in Santiago was not. The beginning is the most difficult, and making the right step at the right time is vital. How I remember those agonizing hours of doubt as a young minister! Where should we start working? How do you reach people for the first time? With no pre-determined plans of how to begin a missionary program, we had but one resource for guidance — prayer. Thus began days of walking and praying through the streets of Santiago. Louise and I would walk through areas of the city of 200,000 praying for direction as to where to begin. We knew where not to start. There were but a few other evangelical efforts in the city, but we surely did not want to intrude into those areas. There were plenty of unchurched peoples, and the preaching of the Gospel is to be a cooperative effort and not a competitive one.

Then, as I felt the direction of our work taking shape, our spirits settled over an area near the harbor of Santiago. It was a basic residential area of the working class, typically dotted with small corner grocers and resounding with the juke boxes of bars placed as thick as two per city block. On the 8th of May, 1955, our first Sunday School opened with 33 children. Louise taught the group she had gleaned from a week of visiting homes in the neighborhood.

A rented building was the beginning of our base church in Cuba. From Sunday School, we progressed to evening services with the parents of the children. This church family was to grow, purchase property, endure a revolution, and stand some 40 years later as a standard of the Christian faith even in the midst of Communist Cuba. "Small beginnings" are indeed not to be despised or taken lightly. Louise taught the children. I read my labored sermons at night. It was a year before a native pastorate became established. So, for that year, I got my practice in with language use and took an "on-the-job" training course in missionary work.

The first work and much of the continuation of the work would depend on women and native Cuban ministry so vital to success. There is no sure foundation in a mission effort based in foreign labor. My task was to begin, to introduce, to help; the church that would develop had to be Cuban through and through. Our task was to begin a Christian ministry and then to work our way out of it. It had been ladies that first walked through the neighborhoods, knocking on doors, dressing children for Sunday School, and walking them to service. During the week, we would visit those homes and talk with parents. Evening services with my guitar and preaching (shared by Louise and myself) would draw a sparse attendance in our first year.

Yet some months of this brought us to a special series of revival services with the stateside team of Rev. Cullen Hicks and Lewellyn Widener, and the nucleus of a Cuban church was born with 22 members. From that number and those workers, an organization would eventually develop that numbered 24 churches, over 40 Sunday Schools, and a strength to stay for over three decades under Communist domination and harassment. Tribute must be paid to those Cubans who founded the church work and remained faithful in service.

Nenita Gonzales came with her children. She was a "pure blood" — very Spanish. "Devoted Christians" well describes Nenita and her six children. As a founding stone in the Cuban church, she was invaluable though her husband was never converted. She would eventually leave Cuba in flight from the Communist rule and, with her sister, would help to establish a thriving church in New York. But, the cost was dear. Her husband was not released from Cuba because of his critical occupation of train engineer. Exiled from home and husband, she stood faithful in Christian service. But as this young mother appeared in services in 1955, none of this tragedy was in her thoughts. Open hearts and a willingness to commit themselves to good works marked these people's lives.

Nenita's sister was a spiritist, attending temples of warlocks and witches. Spiritism was a common worship form to the Cuban culture. Warlocks, mediums and other demonic participants directed basic witchcraft activities. Hut-like temples marked the island. Temples which were kept in private homes were within a short walk of any dwelling. The altars contained a variety of gods with statues of St. Lazarus and the dogs that licked his sores being the most popular. In essence, the worship was a corrupted form of worshipping Catholic saints.

There were evenings when I visited services to observe this corrupt religion. In a single evening, I visited eighteen temples in Santiago and found all in service. Being a young missionary, I felt a need to understand this

19

element of the culture. I fasted and prayed for spiritual strength and set out alone. My physical aloneness was actually dangerous but not nearly so dangerous as the spiritual confrontation that took place. I was challenged openly in services more than once.

"¿Americano, que esta haciendo aqui?" (American, what are you doing here?) "You have no business here," were the defiant words of the temple warlock.

Services were thus frozen in time and ceased until I left the building. It was face-to-face confrontation, the warlock and the missionary. I did not take it in hand to do battle on "his turf." Each encounter left me with a heavy spirit, but with even more determination to press on toward truth for these beloved people as well as for myself.

The most disturbing activities of spiritism involved the children. The tiniest of sons and daughters presented food offerings to rot for three days before statuettes. Then, they returned to digest the food themselves. These children could frequently be seen in paralyzing trances and frenzied dances.

This was the atmosphere and background of many of our converts. Pilar, Nenita's sister, seemed to have but a casual involvement in spiritism, yet the effects were radical. Being sick one evening, Pilar came to service with her sister. As we believed and practiced prayer for the sick, Pilar came and received healing. This experience turned her heart and convinced her of the truth of Christianity. A week later, she was converted and committed herself to Christ. Then the attacks came. Violent headaches would seize her. There was but one relief. The moment she entered the spiritist center, the headaches would stop. It was her only relief. Obviously, spiritual forces had overcome her. "I know the devils by name," she said to me. "I talk to them at night in my room."

As a young minister, I had not encountered this before. I truly did not believe her! It was like some old wives' tales I had heard. Yet, what was I to do? I could not laugh at her nor could I dismiss it since the reality of her suffering was evident and the connection of spiritist worship was clear. Knowing little, but believing in God's wisdom, we prayed. In the simplest of terms, we sought God's help and found it sufficient. Pilar's deliverance from the headaches was instant and the bondage of spirit worship was broken completely. The result was a life long dedication to Christian service.

Leaving one's past behind, as in Pilar's case, is not always easy. Changes cost us and one conversion brought to our home a "miracle." The name "Milagros" is a popular Spanish name meaning "miracles." When this orphan girl of 14 accepted the Lord through our services, her sister literally put her out on the street. She was sent out to the street corner and all her clothes and meager possessions were stacked beside her. What a sight! A frightened young girl standing amidst a small pile of clothing totally lost as to what to do next. When word came to us, Louise and I immediately went to find her. Of course, never did we realize that Milagros would become our unofficial adoptee for the next four years, living in our house, sharing our lives, and becoming our first "daughter." Milagros married a pastor of one of our works later in life. She too fled for the States at the appropriate moment with her two children — again at the cost of family for her husband was never able to follow. One family became two over the years as both remarried in their separate countries. The wedge of Castro broke many things and the wall of

Communism cuts through hearts and families as well as nations.

Other workers were added to the Cuban church effort. People of all backgrounds worked together. The Cuban people were, to some extent, very race conscious at that time, having the blacks, the mixed, and the "pure bloods" who claimed Spanish ancestry. Yet, within the church such differences were ignored. As our family grew, no difference was made. The addition of Eddie, a young black orphan of 12, was beyond a doubt one of our better decisions. The shoe shine boy who came weekly to shine shoes at our door was a street child. On one weekly visit, he asked for sleeping space in our garage as he had lost his place. Eddie's new quarters were quickly put in order, and it became apparent that he was going to be a valuable addition to our home. There was nothing he could not do or learn. I taught him all I knew of building and repair work. As churches were built, it was Eddie that was there to help. Whatever my need, Eddie was my man. Yard work, building, guarding the house in our absence, protecting our possessions in revolutionary times, being my companion in the absence of Louise and Allen — one could ask for no more in a young friend. Thus, our Cuban family changed from time to time but basically the four of us worked together unaware of the trials ahead that would separate us.

"Hugh, I think Elmer needs to make a change, and I would rather see him with you than anyone else." Those words from Robert Hough startled me even as my mind raced back over the record of Elmer Moreira. This young, intelligent and gifted preacher would be an asset to our work, but the policy of transferring workers from one organization to another is a touchy one. Yet, here was my friend Robert telling me that the change was to be made with his approval. Even in church work, personalities do not always fit, and this move was definitely to my benefit. It is truly a supernatural working when such moves can be made to lessen personal frictions without human bitterness and animosity.

This striking young Latin came with education and ability. His songs of worship inspired any crowd. It would be Elmer that would travel to the States with me to encourage support for our work. It would be he who pastored the Santiago church and pushed the work forward. But, it would be Elmer who got caught in the States with me when Fidel's policies became too dangerous for him to return. It would be Elmer who would struggle for a full year to get his wife and child out of Cuba to be with him. And, it would be Elmer who tragically died on an Alabama road, leaving his wife and two sons to struggle for themselves in this life. The days of working side by side with Elmer Moreira became my personal blessing. One becomes a missionary with the thought of giving to others. In this relationship, I became the receiver.

One cannot tell the end from the beginning of a relationship. Doubtless, this is the wisdom of God. Had we seen the tragedies and struggles ahead, would we have worked with the same zeal and fervor? And, yet all is past, it is the accomplishment of those days that stands. A tragic death cannot erase the ministry of the man, his work in translation after coming to the United States, his leadership in stabilization of the Cuban church. His death came on a trip seeking appointment to church work in the country of Honduras — the desire to serve had not dwindled with the rigors of a revolution.

There is talk of sacrifice in the work of missionaries. Those who give of themselves are easy to find in this difficult field of service. Something keeps them going on when others do not. A touch of fire has reached into their hearts that cannot be quenched. This fire reaches every dedicated minister and the missionary convert is certainly no exception. The Apostle Paul once wrote of his confidence that "neither death, nor life, nor angels, nor principalities, nor powers, nor things present, nor things to come ... shall be able to separate us from the love of God." (Romans 8:38) Paul was, of course, correct — but a man named Fidel sure tried his best to separate all that he could.

As laborers in the church became dear friends, at least one became a mortal enemy. The successes of the Cuban people as ministers could fill books: the faithfulness of the Nenitas and Pilars, the dedicated work of Victor Badillo who pastored in Santiago and became an evangelist in Miami after flight from Cuba, the steadfastness of Enrique Ortiz who led the Cuban church in the midst of Communism under Castro until Enrique's death in 1982. But the church work was not without trouble also. No bed of roses is void of thorns and no garden flourishes without the pulling of tares. Even so, the Cuban people and the church work among them was relatively free of the problems common to religious work.

Only twice in the six years of our Cuban work did the body have to take strong disciplinary action with its pastors. Both occasions were the results of that age-old problem of "another woman." Dealing with the situations was not pleasant but neither were they earth shaking. The ruling committee of the church asked for the ministerial licenses in both cases. No ill will was apparent and the sad business was considered unfortunate, but necessary. But, bitterness of the heart is not a visible thing and one of the men committed himself to revenge. Luis Chacon was one of those disciplined and his response would bring my most frightening moments. The revenge he sought would be directed toward me.

3

We Will Stay Forever

Clinics and hospital facilities in other lands are not the same as they are at home. This mountain clinic in Palma Soriano certainly was not a deluxe medical center. Three rooms, a recovery room, and an operating room comprised the total facility. The shutters on the windows had been thrown open to let in the natural light of the sun. Of course, this also allowed free entrance and exit to any insects or other flying creatures that chose to view my illness. Just past the windows, the royal palms spread up the mountainside. It was familiar territory. Our churches spread through these mountains, and we traveled the route often.

The work had begun slowly. First, we opened the work in the city of Santiago which we considered home. In truth, the house was in Santa Maria, a suburb of Santiago but the difference was hardly noticeable. From Santiago, the trail of our missions went across the mountains some 13 miles to the small village of Dos Caminos (Two Ways). We started service in a rented building, actually a large house, equipped to handle church meetings as well as the housing of a native pastor. A trained worker (Carlos Pellon) took charge of these services immediately. Successful planting of churches is all but impossible without dependable local leadership, and we were blessed in that area. Carlos saw rapid growth, from 41 persons to

200 in three months. It was enough to make a young missionary like myself dizzy with excitement.

The work in Dos Caminos began in July of 1956. It began a route of churches that would circle north for 95 miles and then east to the coast, ending back in Santiago. Each community had its own character and no two groups of worshippers were the same. Was I surprised at the adaptability it takes to do the work of a missionary! The first work was hard, but I sort of hoped that further work would just be a matter of repeating the process with a few changes to the individual situation. But, even a land as small as Cuba (the size of a single U.S. state such as Tennessee), the variety of techniques was as endless as the number of villages we worked in . There were times when a work began from a need impressed on my heart and mind while in prayer. In those cases, Louise or I would feel "burdened" about a location or a group of people.

Other times, a knock at the door would reveal some Cuban minister asking, "Rev. Skelton, may I visit with you?" Then, after lengthy discussion, a request might come to work together or to visit with the man's little church or mission. Thus, some works came to us as already functioning churches needing a larger fellowship of believers. And, yes, there are some works that seem to have "just happened." A look backward over those times indicates a Providential guidance in these matters. I am not a proponent of ignorance, but in spiritual work there are times I am sure God finds our ignorance an asset. My not knowing what to do next, left God an opportunity to fill the void with His plans.

Working with individuals concerning their spiritual well-being was ... shall we say "interesting." "I know! I know! We all got a soul. But, I'll worry about that when it comes time to die!" This was the commentary of a 70 year old lady who confessed total unconcern for her personal soul. What response could I make? You just don't say "But, lady, you are 70 now. How long are you going to live?" No, you don't say such things. Just chalk it up to another contradiction of reason, let it puzzle your mind, but keep on going. Next, please.

Establish, preach, train, encourage and let go. That was the pattern for church work. The "let go" is the most difficult part, and it is also the portion so often neglected. Yet, it is vital, vital, VITAL! It is truly the essence of successful church planting. If God can establish me; if He can establish American churches; if He can run a world-wide church, then God can and must become the source of everything you or I try to set up. The job of the missionary is to work himself out of a job. So, establish, preach the Gospel, train workers. But, as these workers grow in wisdom and strength, become the encourager and not the leader. Then, finally, let it go. Leave the work to the local personnel and God. It is amazing how capable they are.

Home visitation is the basis for establishing a completely new work. Thus, the churches often began with women visiting in a new area and my staying home to pray. I thank the Lord for a wife like Louise. She is so good at this work. Louise (like most women) enjoys conversation, and she communicates well in either English or Spanish. Her true interest in people comes through, and she isn't shy about the Lord's interest either. So, for the time of first works, my preaching had to wait on Louise's ministries. After a time of visiting homes, Louise would gradually introduce Sunday School services in the community. My "spiritual" work was most likely involve sweat and muscle aches. It went like this.

Walk through neighborhoods with eyes searching for a building suitable for church work.

"Hola, Señor. What is this building used for? It's all boarded up. Oh, it opens on weekends in the evening for dances — ok. Thanks a lot."

Try another place. Walk, get to know the area. Ahh, there is a really good place. "How much, Señor? Oh, it is a nice building."

"Yes, I see that it needs only a few new shutters and the rats will be no problem to get rid of. How much do you think it is worth?"

"So much, Señor? What if it is for the work of God? Do you think we might get a better price for a church work?"

Negotiate, talk, negotiate. Find a suitable place combined with a suitable owner. Then, work. Clean up the place. Buy lumber. Saw wood. Make benches and a crude pulpit. Fix broken rafters or roof or walls. Don't worry about broken windows — nothing in them to break! And, remember to thank the Lord for those many days watching my father at work.

The knowledge has finally found its place of action. The Sunday School work, now meeting in a home or more likely a neighborhood yard, must be moved to the building. Then, we would gradually work toward weekly services and preaching. Nothing was "overnight" in its developing, but it was the work I was called to do. In the middle of a poor Cuban area of mud houses, surrounded by those totally different in culture and language, operating on too little funds and pressed by personal financial need and family responsibility, sweating over a pile of lumber with a hand saw in hot humid weather, I was completely happy. It was where I was supposed to be, and I was happy in it.

From the work in Santiago and the newly developing church in Dos Caminos, the Cuban conference of churches and missions began to take shape. Eventually the church district would cut a triangle from the southernmost tip of the island. Of course, the roads did not go that way so a circuit trip was not possible without some back tracking. From Santiago on the coast, we went inland 12 miles to Dos Caminos, another 4 miles north to San Luis, and then 50 plus miles northwest to Holguin. Retracing the road back to Santiago, the work then moved east to the Guantanamo Bay area at the end of the island. The total number of works grew with additional Sunday Schools and home studies working out from these churches.

Traveling to visit the areas was a pleasant drive into lush mountain foliage. The farthest church could be reached in three to four hours. Roads were good but carts carrying cane, water, and supplies kept traffic to a slow pace. From the mother church in Santiago, daughter churches arose in Dos Caminos, San Luis, and Holguin. The matter of church planting was generational and the third generation came rapidly. From Santiago came the village missions of Boniato and El Cañon. Dos Caminos produced two additional Sunday Schools in its area. From San Luis, three inner-city Sunday Schools grew. Out of Holguin spread a Concepcion village mission and two inner-city Sunday Schools as well as the Buenaventura church.

Thus, the mother church in Santiago had produced three daughters to the north. They in turn produced a total of 4 grandaughter works and 7 extension Sunday Schools. Within three years, we saw fourth generation churches spread from Buenaventura, our northernmost church. All of this to the north was balanced by the eastern leg of the triangle. Eleven church works marked the road from Santiago to Gauantanamo, some 54 miles eastward. It was a completed district, of 21 church works stretching from the coast 90 miles northward and over 50 miles to the east. We sat where Fidel would come.

By the fall of 1956, we frequently recorded a weekly total in services of more than 400. Our work was showing progress and things seemed to be establishing themselves. In Santiago, Sunday services were supplemented by Tuesday night Bible classes, and from this church came workers to minister in other areas. The family of Gloria Vasquez became pillars of stability in the San Pedrito work some few miles farther. That same year, Sunday Schools in Boniato were drawing over 60 to service just weeks after opening.

The village of El Cañon became a field for mission services. But within a year of the beginning there, revolutionary troubles turned this into a critical area. The bombing of a nearby radio tower there brought home to all the fact that Cuba was indeed a country pressing toward a bloody struggle. Time was short. The need for harvest became urgent.

In El Puerto ("The Door"), there was an effort to step into a room of darkness with the light of the Gospel. This little area of "bohios" along the roadside could hardly be called a village. It was a string of "bohio" huts made of the bark of palm split for the sides. The foot thick thatched roofs of palm fronds were a haven for all things living — lizards, bugs, bats, etc. But this particular area was a center of spiritism. Opposition to our efforts were open and hostile. It has been erroneously assumed that Cuba was primarily a Catholic country. It was rather a pagan land ruled by superstition, magic, witchcraft, and animism. Some spiritist worship was carried out in the sham of a perverted Catholicism, but all Christian effort, Catholic and Protestant, struggled against a common spiritual enemy — animism and Satan worship.

Typical missionary work is seen clearly by a closer look at the church in San Luis. The women began, Sunday School developed, the preacher of record (me) became the assistant. I worked, I gave advice, I encouraged the women, but I also had to wait. Morning services started, mainly for women whose husbands did not object to their absence in the morning when the men were away. Slowly, we expanded to evening services where the men began to take interest. It was then that the missionary became the true pastor and preacher — for a short while. My final goal was to step away and leave local leadership to direct the work.

Old-line culture prevailed. I could not visit homes without Louise while men were at work no matter how many children were present or what the need. But, when those men came to church, they expected to see a man in charge of service. Adapt! Adapt to their style and their culture. After all, our purpose was to bring Christianity, not a new culture. The process was successful over and over again.

With the establishing of youth groups in the church and the coming of native workers to conduct services, my job became one of stepping back to give way to local leadership. How long does it take? Every location was different, but sensitivity to the right timing was essential. No church can remain strong without local foundation. Foreign ministry was never my aim. At San Luis, as everywhere, my work began in the background and to be successful had to end with me in the shadows — supportive but not controlling.

Philosophies are proved by time and reality. The dedication to local leadership held true. The churches became Cuban churches with Cuban pastors and Cuban workers. When "Yankee Go Home!" became the slogan of Cuban politics, our churches stood on strong foundation and the work continued. When the time came that we had to leave, only a pause to mourn the departure of friends marked the time. There was no break in the Christian ministry, no loss in the leadership.

Now, the church at San Luis is also good to look at closely because it showed my finer talents. My guitar playing and singing were adequate. On a scale of 1 to 10, I'd give myself about a 3 ½. But, I shined as a carpenter. In fact, I often became contractor, architect, foreman, and even day laborer as the church took shape. Whatever the need of the day, it was my job to do what I could. God had graciously prepared me for such tasks in the North Georgia hills as a child. And, what I could not do from prior training became an opportunity for on-site education.

The San Luis church was a building of distinction, easily identified by "el torre". The mahogany lattice-work tower stretched upward and outward over people walking past. Downtown, only a block off the main square, it was a building of which I was proud. The kiln-fired bricks were the standard Latin type, flat and broad. Jalousie windows gave it a certain Caribbean look, and the oblong shape of them was definitely modern. The sides remained dark despite the windows because of neighborhood crowding. Only the front windows, marked by my plants and greenery at their base, and the high windows behind the pulpit provided natural light for the church.

Services started at 7:30 p.m. and lasted until 9:00 p.m. or later. The platform was filled with guitars, speakers, and musicians in their hours of worship. People sat on the comfortable wooden benches (Remember, I made them!) while children slept on the floor or played beneath them. Men tired from the day in sugar cane fields filed the left as wives and children sat to the right. The brick walls were covered by stucco plaster on the inside and the exposed rafters, finished timbers rather than rough-hewn, gave spiritual warmth to the building. The church itself reflected the congregation, a strong people of faith. Though only 30 feet wide and slightly deeper, it was overflowing with dedicated worshippers. Both by physical structure and by the character of the people, I found this church a point of pride within me. Carefully, such pride must be channeled. It was not mine, nor were the people mine. But together, God allowed us to construct beauty in this world and in time eternal. At the dedication of the building, some 400 or 500 persons were present. An evangelical witness was being raised in the city and people were taking note.

Other missions sprang up. There was El Artificio and Panadero. In Concepcion, a small work developed when a woman donated land for a mission building. Holguin became an adventure just to visit. Constant stopping was required to register and pass inspection of soldiers on the verge of conflict. A stay there lasted a long time in the memory. The milk of the area had a strangely salty taste, and nights were spent in combat with armies of mosquitoes. Perhaps Fidel's troops took lessons from them.

The growth of the church work to a total of 21 churches and 43 Sunday Schools, clearly indicated a massive hunger for realistic Gospel ministry. The prevalence of ritualistic Catholicism contrasted with voodoo and witchcraft of the basest sort, leaving fertile soil for the seed of practical personal Christianity. But, even as the people responded so readily and zealously, that very spiritual background produced a vacuum of understanding. The drawing in of followers to the message of the Gospel was easy compared to the task of teaching, counseling, and guiding converts into spiritual understanding. And, the job of evangelism is incomplete if it only brings one to the point of decision. There must be a commitment to teach and to care for those seeking to grow in the faith.

Native pastors and teachers had to be recruited and taught. Then as they took over posts of responsibility, they had to be encouraged and counseled. They were eager to learn and their dedication was to be severely tested in the coming days. As storm clouds of politics gathered, the harvest had to be gathered quickly. The courage of the Cuban Christian was to be tested in sufferings of hunger, humiliation, and even imprisonment. Some did not stand, but the majority held fast in the face of opposition. The anchor held in the storm of persecution, and the muffled voice of the Cuban evangelical is still heard today.

As the growth of churches in size and number provides a clear mark of progress, there were other ministries that have no "count" to them. They don't show up on charts or monthly reports. One such ministry was indeed our "first love." Louise's bout with tuberculosis at age 20 gave her a ready burden for visitation and work among the tubercular colony residents of Cuba. The facility was inviting, but few visited. Along the side of the green forested mountain, long low buildings were laid out. An open porch connected the barracks, and the wards were actually very pleasant with the wooden shutters thrown back from spacious windows. This well staffed "institution" was government sponsored and much better than seen in most countries. Yet, all the clean, airy facilities in the world, did not remove the loneliness, the pain, the suffering of disease.

Each week we walked along the porches, stopping to talk with patients who rocked in the open air for hours. On these porches, Louise would play the accordion and I would struggle with the guitar. The sermons were brief — the attention total. For all the medical and physical facilities of this place, the one thing still lacking was the human touch. The fear of tuberculosis was severe, and few visitors dared approach the place. Songs and sermons and conversations from the heart became every much as refreshing as the mountain breezes or the view of coconut trees and wild orchids on the hillside. Whatever the beauty or the provision of the Lord, people long for love and communication with other people. And no punishment is so severe as separation from the human touch — unless it be separation from the spirit of God.

Visits to this facility led us to another — our most emotionally rewarding. Each weekend throughout our years in Cuba, we worked in the leper colony also. It lay some 14 miles down the coast, and government permission was required to visit such places. Once that approval was gained, we were at total liberty among these distressed people. "Fear and trembling" adequately describe our first approach to the camp. Being rather ignorant about leprosy, we spent a great deal of time in preparatory prayer on those first visits — we were praying we wouldn't "catch" leprosy. That, of course, was not too likely; however, the prayer did prepare us with hearts tender toward the beauty of these needy people. Here lived the rejects of society — outcasts through no fault of their own. They starved for the dignity of human relationships. I would preach during each visit, and then Louise and I visited among the people. Music, small gifts, and simple friendships took on meaningful wealth to these whom the public ostracized.

Of course, we learned a lot too. Mostly I learned that a person can be terribly ignorant of a thing and never learn better if he stands off and looks at it. The courage to step up and deal with the unknown brings understanding, wisdom, and possibly untold blessing. My ignorance of leprosy was monumental, but because of our willingness to step in, we did learn that it was not so dangerous after all. Basic caution is sufficient to protect most people since contact with open sores is the most common manner of transmission. We soon lost all misgivings about contact with those of the leper colony, and found a delight in their friendships that will last forever.

Still, the sight and the smell of leprosy as an active disease, never leaves one's memory. The blindness, the sores, the total devastation of the human body left us unable to approach a meal for hours and sometimes days after a visit. It is no wonder that the Old Testament Scriptures choose this disease to teach of the degenerating of the spirit through sin. Our visits to the lepers and to the tubercular patients became a permanent part of our Cuban experience. There we found friends and Christian fellowship. Those marked "unclean" are not always so. Likewise, the noble work of missions, church planting, and the growth of ministry among the well is little more than a focus of that same love toward the debilitating forces of sin and evil. All without Christ are as crippled as the partially limbed leper — perhaps more so.

4

Between the Battle Lines

"Early in the morning of the last day of November, Castro's forces struck in Santiago Cuba, the island's second city, 500 miles east of Havana. Wearing uniforms like the Cuban Army's and arm bands inscribed "26 de Julio" (the date of an unsuccessful uprising in 1953), some 200 civilians attacked two police stations, apparently hoping to set off a general revolt."

~~ Newsweek Magazine, p.56, Dec. 17, 1956

To say we lived in the midst of the revolution is to put it mildly. Oriente Province was the home of Fidel. His first attempt to take over the barracks of the military forces was in Santiago at the Cuartel Moncado. His landing on the "Gramma" on December 2, 1956, was as close to Santiago as he could get the ship. The forerunner to his landing was my first brush with the fighting and with the death that was to surround us in coming years. The incident reported above by Newsweek Magazine made my November 30, 1956, a little different from other Friday mornings.

A trip to the Post Office was not unusual. There was always the hope of mail from home — maybe even a package. In the center of town, the stucco structure was open in the middle with a "dog run" type opening. Business was carried on inside with easy access to streets at either end. I parked the old '54 Chevrolet station wagon and strolled in. But, the "companeros" of Fidel were waiting for his return from exile and began their move to let the world know a revolution was beginning in Cuba. The firing of guns startled me and all the other patrons. It was dive for cover of any kind. I crouched behind the mail stacks. The one and a half hours passed minute by minute — an eternity of 90 minutes.

Fear is indescribable and unreasonable. On one hand, the heart pounds and one's breathing becomes difficult. Yet, the mind slows and takes in every detail. Thoughts become busy with nonsense things like the appearance of the mail stacks, how high they are, what is written on the sacks. The features of the floor become fascinating so the mind will remain focused on something tangible and rational. I began counting the spurts of gunfire as though keeping track of them would make them less harmful. There was an incessant need to keep the mind occupied; as long as you can think, you know you are still alive. The opposing forces were stationed at either end of the building and our open walkway through the Post Office was the bullet zone. And there was nothing to do — nothing to do but crouch and pray.

And then the shooting stopped. Simply stopped. Revolutionaries and government troopers scurried away and a frightening silence took over. How simple! Just get up, straighten yourself a little, pick up your things and go. In the midst of terror, we returned to the safety of rote behavior. So, I walked out of the Post Office, looked around carefully, walked to the car and drove home.

Outwardly, I did the normal natural thing. Inwardly, all of my being shook. Yes, I have been afraid. And that fear did not leave quickly, nor did it make the next time I encountered gunfire one iota less frightening. That experience was to be repeated many times in the coming years. Oh, it was not in the same place, or the same people, but it was the same encounter with death and war. The firing all sounded alike. It brought that same paralyzing fear. We would later become almost accustomed to the sounds of shooting, but the fears were just better controlled and buried within us. But, the terror never went away.

As I drove away from that first battle, I pulled past a car just ahead of me on the street. The driver was motionless. The large bullet hole in his forehead was unmistakable. Just as the sounds of war would become familiar but not comfortable, so would the sights. My reaction to them never came short of terror and nausea. In the name of political ideologies, in the search for power, in man's struggle to better life by his own efforts, life and the price of life become unbelievably low. Human suffering was the price of the Cuban Revolution, but it was always someone else's suffering. Fidel made the forces and the supporters of Batista pay the cost. Batista made the followers of Fidel pay. And the innocent paid both sides. Exacting the price was the call of each side in this war. Paying the price was not the style of either leader.

The war "escalated" — what a nice way to say things became truly horrible. Castro's forces hid in the mountains of Oriente Province. In reality, the war was fought around our house. Two armies battled back and forth. The months of shelling became unbearable — and yet one cannot stop the noises nor quit the living. Constant prayer was our means of safety and sanity.

In Sta. Maria, we were blessed with a home covered by a 5-inch concrete roof. That meant that as soon as the sounds of battle started, we were also blessed with visitors. Our home became the neighborhood rallying place for it was the safest place in town. Of course, we did lose a portion of the garage to explosives and a neighbor's yard gained a swimming-pool sized hole from rocket fire.

The desire to stay with our Cuban friends struggled with our need for security and the responsibility a husband and father feels to keep his family from danger. Decisions at this time were crucial, and they were certainly not easy. Crouching with fear in the center of the house while rockets whistled overhead was far from pleasant. However, looking up to see Louise and four-year old Allen tormented by fear strained my mental abilities to their limit. The American Consul had begun to advise our leaving.

The sights of those days are never forgotten. They don't come in nightmares, but rather in open daylight. For years, my mind had sudden images of the suffering. The stories, the pictures, even the events themselves seem unspeakable yet they were real and visible. Men were buried alive; nails were driven into their hands and their mouths were sewn shut with wire. Women were found nailed onto walls. A boy and his bicycle were found buried together. Finger nails and eyes were extracted. Who was responsible? It was the result of hatred and inhumanity in the name of "liberty" or "justice" whichever you choose. It was a time of darkness and the oppression of that darkness colored every day and almost every thought. For us, the war was a struggle like that of the Apostle Paul when he noted, "We wrestle not against flesh and blood, but against principalities and powers of darkness..." (Ephesians 6:12)

In the last moments of the Batista reign (late 1958), Robert and Velda came down from Palma Soriano in a private plane. The thirty-mile trip put these friends in a safer place since the mountains were to prove the pivotal strength for Fidel's forces. And, we were glad to have company in the house. Though we did not know it at that

42

time, when Santiago fell, the Revolution would be won. There in Santiago (actually in the suburb of Sta. Maria), the Hough's sought safety in a city with its main highway cut off by rebel forces for seven weeks. Our position in the suburb was just northwest of the city toward the major fighting areas. Food supplies were low and we were already prepared for evacuation of the house on short notice. Even in such troubled times, we managed some jubilation at the arrival of friends and the prospect of someone to share the hours and fears.

But then, Robert is not a person to sit still. On December 8, 1958, daylight found the two of us starting out on foot to "see the sights" of the Revolution. That was not our true purpose, of course, and no one would have been so flippant as to think of a pleasure excursion at this point. Robert and I left with literature to distribute to the soldiers. Each of us carried a grocery bag stacked with tracts and Gospel messages printed in Spanish. And, being good Americans, we had our cameras inconspicuously tucked away also. The sixteen-mile hike to La Maya was to be my most memorable missionary journey in Cuba though I certainly did not know it at the time.

From Sta. Maria to Boniato was relatively easy. Crossing the lines beyond was a bit more frightening. Batista's soldiers were encamped on the outskirts of Boniato. We first had to secure permission from their Commander to cross over their lines into "no man's land." The total distance was no more than a mile. Two armies faced one another over this strip that any other time would be considered a nice brisk morning walk. Robert and I got our permission, took a deep breath, gathered up our nerves and started out. It was our intent to give testimony about Christ and to minister to soldiers of both sides. The

43

wounded and dying were evident, and we especially wished to minister to them. As we left the uneasy safety of the Batista Camp, the mile before seemed to widen.

Near Castro's battle lines, a rider on horseback approached us. He was a soldier from Castro's army, and his approach quickened our hearts. "Why are you here? What do you want?" Our explanation was direct and truthful. "We are ministers of the Gospel seeking to distribute literature to your soldiers." How easily he accepted our words and escorted us the remaining distance to the Commander in charge of the area, a Lt. Santiago. After more discussion, we were given written permission to minister and distribute literature among the troops. Wonderful! We were feeling safer — as safe as a piece of paper can make you feel in the midst of bullets.

Our ministry began and our safety net showed immediate flaws. The planes of Batista could not read our papers from the air as they strafed the area with bullets. What must have been minutes, seemed like hours. We huddled behind a cement wall with dozens of others. Heroes we were not as we grouped ourselves with the odd mixture of soldiers, civilians, and children. As we waited for more planes, bulldozers began to cut ditches across the highway as a deterrent to tanks. NOISE! NOISE! NOISE! It was unbearable and seemingly unreal.

But, it did come to an end. The planes left and noise gradually changed into a dull roar of machinery and distant rocket fire. People returned to their tasks as Robert and I continued our ministry down the semi-destroyed highway of La Maya. It was another couple of hours to El Cristo. This little town named for the Christ, the Peacemaker, was in rubble. In the burning and bombing of the area, some 200 soldiers had been killed in the Cuartel.

As we traveled further, at least three small villages were found in this same condition. The smoldering buildings showed signs that they still burned deep within the heaped destruction. The day became a tired day, and the whole world seemed to be stifled with smoke and ash.

La Maya was our destination, and it had been Castro's goal only hours earlier. A major battle the day before had given him the city at 1:00 p.m. The view that rose to meet us was the saddest I have ever seen. This city in the beautiful Sierra Maestra mountains was no more. Total destruction had been Fidel's plan. People who had fled during the battle for the city were returning in lines. They filed out of the mountains in never-ending lines to sift through the ashes of what had once been homes. Women knelt in tears as their husbands sifted the ashes by hand looking for some remnant of a home, of a dish, of a reminder of the life that had existed just the day before. Anything of value would help them rebuild. Any memento of the past was worth cries of delight. But there were few cries of delight and few discoveries. Men stood dazed by the hopelessness of the situation, and soldiers patrolled the streets. The city was reduced to jumbles of nothingness. We walked the streets in sadness, carefully stepping around the mounds of dirt that dotted the streets. Each small concave mound was a hastily thrown dirt cover for some person's body. The cost of war was being paid by a people who wanted to live in peace. A lifetime of possessions had disappeared with the political ambitions of two men. Batista or Castro — either side would cost these people all they owned.

It was as we began the trip back to Santiago that I became aware of the blisters on my feet. Steps became painful. The smoke of the ruins around us seemed to burn into my shoes. The scars left on my heart were not physical, but they would never be erased. Humans destroy other humans so like themselves in the name of freedom, or truth, or some principle dear to the heart. Where but in war is there found so great a contradiction of the Christian message? Christ taught the laying down of one's life for another, the giving of His life for truth. Man's is to take one life for another, to take lives to insure truth and freedom.

On the return trip, we stopped by the headquarters of Huber Matos, one of Castro's true heroes. He fought as a compatriot truly believing that Communism played no part in this Revolution. He would face unkindly treatment at the hands of this new government for which he had fought so fiercely — but there was no thought of that now. This chief decision maker, later jailed by Castro for refusing to embrace Communism, was not present, but we did speak with his lieutenant in charge. This leader of the Revolution knew all about us. His words turned my heart cold.

"I know who you are. You are the Americans who live in Sta. Maria with the American flag on your house. You should leave immediately. Evacuate the city. Santiago is surrounded by 10,000 rebel soldiers, and it will be burned as La Maya was burned if necessary. Your home is in the direct line of fire. I advise you, my friend, leave quickly."

The words echoed in our heads as we continued homeward. The truth was clear. The home we loved was now a place of danger. That heavy roof would no longer be sufficient protection. We had kept the flag flying as a hope of sympathy from either side. The last few miles to Sta. Maria came fast to our weary feet. By 8:00 p.m, we found ourselves with celebrating families, happy to see us safe. First need, a foot soaking — one full hour! Then, a warm and welcome meal greeted us. I did manage to marry one of the best cooks on earth! There was much to tell, a lot of conversation, and also a lot to do.

We took the soldier's warning to heart. An early departure was planned for the next morning. The day had taken us many miles. We ministered to hundreds. Secret cameras with forbidden pictures were in the bottom of our bags. Indelible memories and sounds pierced our brains. I had been to La Maya, and I had seen the reality of this time. Tomorrow was the time to leave it behind. Our work for now was finished. We could go no further.

We flew from Santiago to the United States the next day. The small band of the Hough family, Louise, little Allen, and myself did not travel in delight. But, we did travel in gratitude for our lives. Thus, I missed 20 days of the Cuban Revolution for it was 20 days until the island fell and stability under Fidel Castro appeared. The destruction of La Maya did not come to Santiago.

The rebels were prepared to move when a Baptist minister of Santiago was able to negotiate a surrender of the city that assured the safety of the people. From that surrender, the war was really over. Castro had a clear march on to the capital of Havana. The resistance to his forces folded. Santiago proved to be the final "straw." Cuba had fallen. "Long live Fidel Castro!" A new era was starting.

When word reached us, we prepared for an immediate return to our home in Sta. Maria. Why? Because it was our home; it was where we belonged. We prepared to continue our church work with hopes of better days, of democracy, of greater liberty and of a better life for our beloved Cuban people. As a family, we would see two more years on that beautiful island under the leadership of Fidel Castro. We had two more years, but no realization of the struggle and the dangers that faced us in that time. Our love and friendships with the people would not diminish, but the golden prospects for democracy and liberty tarnished and turned to empty tinkling brass.

In our early years there, the Cuban economy was vastly divided. There were the wealthy and the poor. Those of wealth enjoyed the privileges of large houses, beachside apartments, servants, and the Isle of Pines Resort. The poor searched for work and lived in crowded homes or slept in doorways. Work could be made. One old gentleman spent his days filling holes in the road between Sta. Maria and Santiago proper. For this, he received tips from those of us who were glad to see one less bounce or two. Conditions such as these developed an undercurrent of unrest in the people. They did not have to be taught to hate their present conditions when Fidel made his move. The discontent was there for him to use.

"I really think you're wrong, Rene." How many times had I argued the point with this bright young banker. The Batista regime had robbed the people and had lined the pockets of the vultures. The young revolutionist with his fatigue uniform and his "macho" beard looked like a star of hope on the horizon. Yes, I too was convinced that he brought a better way. The platform of reform put forth by Fidel Castro was all the people could dream about. He promised freedom, food, housing, elections, and the right to govern. It could not be criticized. Still, even then, some saw further. As an artist and banker, Rene Longe saw further than I did. He declared from the first, "He is

Communist, and he will take the country that way. Just you wait and see."

But in those first months of the change, I continued to disagree with my neighbor. I was wrong — but I was in good company. From conversations with and knowledge of those who fought with Fidel, there is no doubt that the majority of them were also deceived. He was that "Master of Deceit". Fidel is, if nothing else, a highly intelligent man. Coupled with that intelligence is a power of persuasion that could perhaps rival a Hitler. Using the honest heroes of his country such as Cienfuegos and Huber Matos, he won a war and the hearts of the people. Then in a short time, no more than two years, he completely consolidated the power of the country in his own hands. Those who brought him to power began to fall silently into graves and prison cells.

Cienfuegos disappeared. Simply disappeared! What happened to him is pure guess, but he opposed the turn to Communism and could not be left to stand against it. His influence with the people and his reputation of integrity was too great to battle in public. Huber Matos spent some 20 years in prison. He tells his story in a book of his own as well as in Reader's Digest, April, 1980. How he survived is beyond anyone's imagination and certainly exceeded the wildest expectations of Fidel. Yet, the inner strength of the man held his physical body from death, and his spirit refused to let him die in the filth of Havana dungeons.

Once Fidel gained power and the purge of Batista's followers was completed in bloody fashion, there came a second blood bath. Before outsiders realized it, Communist "advisors", weapons, and even troops began to pour onto the island. My photographs taken as early as 1959 show these movements in the mountain regions. My own report to the American Consulate at great risk of life was shoved in a trash can and I was told, "It is not our business. We are to remain neutral." To accomplish the switch from democratic revolution to Communist takeover, many had to be removed. Literally hundreds of those who fought for Castro were shot. The sound of rapid fire still rings in my ears from that day when 200 revolutionary soldiers were lined up and shot down by their former comrades in arms because they would not go on marching to the left, the left, the left.

Americans became the target of all resentment. If there had not been work under Batista, it was the Americans' fault. If crops had been bad, it was due to some American influence. From the third month of Fidel's rule, open anti-American propaganda prevailed. Signs appeared everywhere. And the constant cry of "Yankee, go home!" echoed in our ears. Still, most of us worked on. Those who had economic involvement in Cuba weighed their chances and decided how long they could stay. Those of us with a dedication to task rather than material goals gave little heed to the warnings. We assumed — wrongly assumed — that since our purposes were non-political and our work humanitarian, we had no part in the changes of government. Even when the newspaper announced that all Americans had 48 hours to leave the island of Cuba, most missionaries received the news with little more than a comment or two.

The coming weeks and months would begin to bring the truth. Gradually, we became aware that we were not immune from the "Yankee hate." Every rise to personal power must come with a scapegoat to trod under foot and in Cuba it would be the American. Unlike the message of Christianity that says love Me and love all mankind, human power rises on the idea of love me more because you hate others so much. Fidel played this ploy to its best. Love Fidel and the Revolution; hate the past and the American. To be a "true Cuban", one had to reject all that was American. It worked. The fires of hate burned so brightly that Fidel was idolized. He could do no wrong and say no wrong. The affection became an unreasoned frenzy. The idol god was raised. Fidel became their Saviour.

We carried the same hopes as the Cuban people in those days. Castro would lead us into democracy, freedom and a better life for the common people. We continued to work as usual with the churches. Our plans for the farm at Boniato were becoming a reality. This mountain retreat of seven acres had been purchased at $250 per acre. Through the years, a caretaker kept the farm in working order with bananas, coconuts, sweet potatoes, and peanuts in abundance. Well, not in saleable abundance. It seems that when sale time came around, the products would be mysteriously "stolen" by mountain thieves — or some other disaster would keep them from market. Since the main goal was not financial gain, we ignored the obvious and reaped the benefits of fresh fruits and vegetables sufficient for our own use. The Boniato farm was our future dream. A large church was under construction with living quarters for Louise, Allen, and myself on the second floor. A lifetime of living and working in Cuba—the dream was soon shattered.

Reality was apparent within three months of Fidel's victory. He consolidated power quickly under his own iron fist. Political control was established; all major opposition destroyed. A next step was nationalization of industry — control of jobs. The sugar cane factories, Cuba's major industry, came under government control. Factory owners were simply moved out at gunpoint and government leadership was installed. Communist philosophy was becoming rapidly clear.

The next move was to control the people. Laws were passed to prohibit people from moving their residences. This gave the government an immediate knowledge of where to find individuals. The buying and selling of property was thus restricted. Fidel was tightening his hold, drawing tighter and tighter the hangman's rope.

Property control would eventually give Castro power over churches. In the philosophy of Communism, rules would come that gave property to whoever lived on it. Thus, our churches would become the property of the pastor living in the building. In most cases, our people made no such move to take the building but permitted the church to retain ownership. At Dos Caminos, the pastor moved swiftly to claim his home. He continued the church work but as his own personal property. In other cases, the government simply forced takeovers. At Concepcion and Boniato, non-Christian families were moved into the church buildings and given ownership because of the "public need for housing." It was not the open attack of "destroy the churches," but rather a sly maneuver to put the property to better use for the "good of the people." Of course, all of this was in the future. For now, all seemed to be only slightly abnormal.

It was during these months that I became aware of Communist military personnel on the island. Into the mountainous end, near Santiago, rumor of foreign soldiers began to circulate. But, we were Americans; we were "NEUTRAL." That was the word repeatedly given to me by the official American presence in Santiago. I carried the document with fear. The paper burned hot in my hands. I shoved it up under the dashboard in fear and traveled as directly to the American offices as I could. When my neighbor had brought the report, I had certainly not wanted it. But, then, who but an American could present the evidence?

The eastern point of the island provided the perfect place for naval maneuvering. As the American Navy held their parcel of land at Guantanamo Bay, submarines were dropping off Czech troops just a few miles away to hide in the mountains awaiting Fidel's call. My Cuban neighbor traveled the area often, selling drugs for a pharmaceutical company and serving patients as a registered nurse. The papers he brought to my home were detailed — a full disclosure of the Communist presence. Even more important was the proof that they had broken the communication code used by American intelligence. He asked that I deliver it to U. S. officials for the sake of the countries, his and mine. Politics is not my line of work nor my interest. Yet, I could not refuse that which was thrust into my hands.

As the car rattled into town, I was past nervous. There was no strength in me. I was certain everyone was watching me. The car was parked, and I walked in the offices to talk with a man I had met many times before. Placing the report on his desk, I sat in silence while he read.

"It is impossible. It cannot be broken!" His voice rose.

Then he became clear and calm, almost as if reading a directive, "We, as Americans, are maintaining a neutral position in this conflict. You as an American and as a minister are not to permit yourself to become involved in the inner politics of this nation."

And with that, he tossed the papers into a nearby trash can. It was the end of the conversation. American intelligence was now an open book to the Communists. It was "impossible" and yet those documents were undeniable proof of the fact. But, we were "neutral". We were not to get involved. And so I walked away.

The Communist troops continued to come. We as Americans remained "neutral". And, my friend with the report from the mountains soon fled for his life seeking refuge through the Guantanamo Naval Base and American territory. The sequence of events in this period is difficult. It all runs together in the mass of intense emotion. On one hand, things were normal. We still traveled weekly into the mountains to work with church people. The countryside changed little on the surface.

While Castro and Batista battled, I fought the bats and rats of Buenaventura. What a time! An evening with the country folk turned into a nightmare and a shopping trip for a new mattress. As I lay down to sleep, there was movement under me, not the sensation of movement but real movement. Rats ran under and inside the mattress. My presence on top was all that kept them from that part. Almost the moment I realized the problem there, bombers began to dive from the ceiling. Were they birds? No, bats! Here I was caught in the middle of another war—rats below and bats above. Another delightful evening at the "Buenaventura Hilton". The family stood in amusement at dawn as I dragged the mattress into the yard and set fire. What's the big deal? Only a few rats. They were happy with the new mattress I purchased to replace my burned one.

So the two years under Fidel's rule were like that. Business went as usual and yet it didn't. We still showered in the back yard of Cuban homes such as that one in Buenaventura. Forget modesty. The little three-foot cubicle covered the necessities from the knees to the shoulders, one and one-half foot of privacy from top to bottom. Fortunately, I am not a tall man. Tilt the shower bucket overhead for a cold gush, soap down, then try for another tilt of the bucket. It was the common lifestyle of the mountain villages. Every neighbor could see the shower stall, but then we could see theirs also.

Things did not change among the people we knew. There was the same friendliness, the same acceptance among our neighbors, our church friends, the people where we shopped. Only from the military and the university student did we begin to see animosity. The "Yankee, go home!" became open in shouts, in wall writings, in open taunts. And yet, there was no feeling of physical fear.

Never, during the post-revolutionary time, did we fear for our lives. Yes, the psychological harassment was there. An increase in military confrontation was evident. Don't leave home without your identity papers. Travel was slowed by the constant military checks. It was difficult to get ten miles out of town without being stopped for a search and identification procedure.

In those instances verbal abuse toward Americans began to surface more and more. The smiles and politeness of years past were replaced by sneers and curses among the "soldados" along the road. Our spirits began to realize the end was near before we ever accepted it in our thoughts. The stress showed in Louise first. We awoke to her terrible hemorrhaging in the night. The year of psychological and emotional stress had broken her body inwardly and the tubercular germ again attacked. At the time though, all we knew was that there was a serious problem. A hasty morning trip to the doctor brought the advice that she be taken to the United States IMMEDIATELY. That meant as soon as it could be arranged. Our neighbor, the nurse and pharmaceutical salesman, came in daily to give medication. For two weeks, we dealt with the struggle to get Louise to an American hospital. The Red Cross was unable to help. Her brother flew in to try to help. He took Allen back with him. Then, Louise and I finally made the flight to Atlanta. We flew through storms much like that first one when we had first come on a ferry boat as man and wife. Neither she nor I realized at the time that it was her last trip from Cuba. We came together in a storm, and we left together in a storm.

An ambulance waited at the Atlanta airport to transport her to St. Joseph's hospital. It was diagnosed as a stress relapse of the tubercular germ. Recommendation: Surgical lobectomy to remove the upper right lobe of one lung. Louise was not ready for a decision of this type, so it was agreed that she could go home to North Georgia for rest and time to consider the surgery. Some time at home in the care of her mother, rest among friends, and prayer would prepare her for whatever was to come. As soon as she was settled there, I returned to Cuba. Things were worsening there.

And, here I am — preparing to leave Palma Soriano and three days of sickness. I still can barely move. My arrival back on the island was normal; the trip up to Palma to visit Robert and Velda was normal; my sudden appendicitis attack and surgery were not normal. Louise lies in a North Georgia mountain farm home facing critical surgery, and I lie in a Cuban mountain clinic near death from non-sterile faulty surgery. I do indeed wonder if our sicknesses are not messages of the body to brains that are slow to comprehend. We are coming to the end in Cuba and are resisting the flood of the enemy in that country with all our spirits. But, my body seeks to draw us out of the danger. We would have likely stayed to the death, but God had other plans.

The trip back home is a flood of pain and semi-consciousness. A young Methodist missionary comes to my rescue offering to drive me the entire 1,500 miles. Robert and Velda prepare a bed in the back of the station wagon and the journey out of the mountains begins. Every bump in the road, every roll of the ferry boat, every stop at a traffic light from Key West, Florida, to Cleveland, Georgia, is felt. The depths of despair are in the scene of that country yard. As we roll to a stop, I raise my head to see a wife pained and weakened on the front porch. We are quite a pair. Neither much help to the other, but we are together again. The pain of the mountain clinic is behind me as I sleep on clean sheets in a warm house with medical help only a phone call away. But, the story of Cuba is not finished yet.

5

Cuba Libre!

Under the wonderful cooking and the care of Louise's mother in Georgia, I recovered rather rapidly. Louise worsened. The surgery was scheduled for early September in Atlanta. It went well, and she soon returned home for recovery. It was obviously time for me to go back to Cuba. We never questioned it. Time was short there, and we were beginning to see the "handwriting on the wall", but that was where I should be. It was the last trip.

In late September, 1960, I flew back knowing that I must clear things for leaving at a moment's notice. At the Havana airport, I made reservations back to the States as a precautionary measure. The earliest return possible was my request. That would be three months away — December 19th. No matter. It was fine. I really doubted I would use it anyway. Just a reservation to keep in case I needed it.

Back to Santiago without a car, Robert Hough and I took up bachelorhood. His family had left by now, so we continued our work together from the house in Sta. Maria. I began selling things slowly. Since the law now said no one could move, we had to sell things in the house and let people come carry it away. We sold off most of the things and literally lived out of suitcases. The bed was still there — sold with the agreement it was to be "picked up" after I left. A major need was to prepare the Cuban church to survive on its own. Fortunately, the local leadership was strong and we saw this as no problem. But, there were details of property and administration to strengthen and clarify.

It was a labor of love and both Robert and I enjoyed the long hot days visiting with our Christian brethren. On one of those normal days of bus trips into the country, we walked back home tired but pleased. It was the end without warning. I would never again visit those friends. No time for "good-bye" messages. No last service together. No prayer of fellowship and God speed. The crowd outside the house was noisy. Something had excited the entire neighborhood. Several ran to me as we walked the few hundred yards from the bus stop, weeping and hugging me. They propelled us to the doorway and the summons attached was clear.

"Hermano, the soldiers came. You will be killed, Señor! It is danger — danger."

The paper on the door was clear. "You are under arrest ... under no circumstances are you to leave the island of Cuba ... appearance before a federal judge commanded at 10:00 a.m., December 19."

My options were closing fast. Wherein was the wisdom of the Lord? Do I go to meet the judge and face the charges? What else can I do? As an American, spy charges against me would not go easy. I sat in the home of a neighbor, the one with whom I had argued that Fidel was not a Communist, and we talked. Rene had a personal friend on the judge's staff. We gathered our suitcases from the house and drove to visit the friend. He was not delicate about his answer.

"Señor, I can lose my head for the advice I am about to give. You must leave. Try for your flight to the U.S. You have nothing to lose by trying."

Yes, there was the flight out. The reservations taken some months earlier in Havana were for December 19, 1960. I do not, despite modern scepticism, doubt the hand of God when I remember those plane reservations. I was due before the judge on December 19. I was due on a flight to Miami on December 19. Which one would I choose? To be arrested in flight from the summons could be no worse than answering it in a contrived court. A friend drove me to the Santiago airport where he was able to smuggle me onto the next flight to Havana. My advantage was that no government official would dream I could get out so quickly.

There were no farewells, no parting looks over the city, just get on the plane and go. It was a race now — time was the critical factor. I lost all concern with things and gave myself to running.

As I entered the Havana airport, a muscular young man in a black leather jacket moved behind me. All night and into the next afternoon, he never lost sight of me. I assume his assignment was the next American that came in and not Hugh Skelton in particular. This "secret police" personnel kept close account of me, but never realized my secret of the summons on the door in Santiago.

The time in the airport was an eternity. It was hot. It was crowded. Every person was taut with nervousness. Twice we were taken into a large room. Crowds of people seeking to leave were noisily trying to cover their frustration. On two occasions, we were interviewed individually. They were not polite.

"Pigs!" "Stupid capitalist!"

No one bothered to talk behind our backs. They were direct face-to-face insults. Repeatedly the luggage was searched and left in disarray. The room was filled with

30 or 40 people awaiting that December 19, afternoon flight to Miami. I was too frightened to notice detail. It all runs into a blur of crowds, noise, and confusion. The only sound that mattered finally came.

"Board the plane."

Freedom was on the way. We settled into the plane and began to move onto the runway. No noise! The engine ceased to whir. We had stopped, and with that stop, my weakened heart fell. Two soldiers approached in their khaki fatigues, revolutionary beards, and military weapons. As they boarded, absolute silence fell. Every eye was riveted on the two intruders. Surely, every heart stopped in that moment. A name was called — not mine. A hand was raised — to the right? Just a bit forward? The soldiers motioned the gentleman forward and escorted him politely from the plane. No comment; no explanations. The engines began to roar again as though nothing had happened. No voice of question spoke out. No buzz of conversation over the loss of a passenger ensued. Speculation about the matter never came. Each of us just sat quietly, washed by waves of relief. I felt it too. They had not come for me. I was not being detained. I still had a chance.

Slowly, the plane started to move. Speed increased. Then, the DC-10 ran faster and faster into the wind. We rose from the ground. We were airborne. We were off the ground. My beloved Cuba was shrinking below me. Home awaited. Physical pain gripped my heart as the conflict touched my innermost being.

"Cuba libre!" "Cuba libre!" "Free Cuba!" "Free Cuba!" It had been the cry of the Revolution. As tears began to fall from my eyes, it was the cry of my heart. I cried in relief for I was to be free. I wept in despair for I left those I loved. The Cuban people went from Batista to Castro — from bondage to bondage. They would not find the dream of freedom, even as no people can find it through politics and governments. Liberty is not contained in documents, or programs, or revolutions, or heroic leaders. True freedom exists only in the individual heart and spirit. As I looked back on the fading island knowing my own personal freedom was assured, the reminder of my calling in life pressed through the chaos. It is the freedom of the spirit that I must proclaim, and the freedom of my beloved Cuban friends that is ever to be my prayer.

"Cuba libre!" "Cuba libre!" Yes, Lord, I pray, "Cuba libre!"

L to R: (p. 64) Baby Hugh, Dad & Mom, rabbit boy, Hugh and Dorothy, wedding day.
(p. 65) Preaching, teaching, scouting, college days.

L to R: (p. 66) Palma Soriano, the young preacher, the family, revolutionary soldiers.
(p. 67) ministry to the rebels, among the dead, the destruction of war.

Part II
On the Edge of a Miracle

On the Edge
After Cuba
Latin American Expansion
Other Horizons

6

On the Edge

It was 5:00 on a crisp morning in the high mountains of Guatemala. The 5:30 bus was just ahead as Rev. Larry Jaques and I set out for Guatemala City. But, in a land where nearly all things are late, we stared at the tail lights of the departing bus. It had been 30 minutes early today. What would we do about that plane for home that left this afternoon? Knowing we had a 4-5 hour trip just to get to the airport, Larry looked at me and said, "I believe you live on the edge of a crisis." I thought a moment and responded, "No, I don't life on the edge of a crisis. I live on the edge of a miracle."

We turned to find some elderly men sitting in the park. A short conversation revealed that there was indeed another bus station in the city. We reached the station just in time to catch a bus loading passengers.

"Is this a bus to Guatemala city?"

"Guatemala City, it is."

"Do you have seats available?"

"Only two."

We needed "only two", and our miracle for that day got us into the city 30 minutes earlier than planned.

Of course, it wasn't our first miracle for that trip. We had started out in Atlanta without Larry's passport. He had left it home and with no time to retrieve it, we hurried toward our boarding gate with courage and a prayer. "Trust God," I told him. "We'll make it through." I also advised him to stay as close to me as possible when we reached Mexico City and the customs check. As usual, my papers were checked and the two of us walked past the officials without his being noticed. Was he invisible?

In Guatemala, the same things occurred. I was checked; Larry was not even noticed. Indeed, I have always stood on a critical edge. But, I choose to see it as the edge of a miracle. One step of faith leads not to a fall into destruction, but rather onto a roadway of opportunity revealed step by step. My life began on that edge. With the doctor's pronouncement that I was a "dead child" at birth, the string of miracles began.

Through those early years of struggle to live, I was being prepared for a future I could not have imagined. The interests of my youth laid a foundation to my life's work in missions. As a youngster, I was unable to participate in any school athletics because of my bad heart. Even recreational activities such as swimming were strictly forbidden by the doctor. As a result, scouting became my passion . From age 9 as a Cub Scout until my second year of college, I involved myself in accomplishment though the Boy Scout Organization rising to level of Eagle Scout, Double Silver Palm.   This process brought me into extensive public speaking in promotion of the Boy Scouts throughout the southeastern states as well as stint as scouting reporter for the Gainesville Times. It was perfect training for long-term planning on the mission field and constant preaching.

Scouting included training as an Air Scout where I took my first flight with absolutely no idea that I would eventually fly over 3 million miles in my future work. The extensive camping was another area of training that included a total of 50 nights in the north Georgia mountains. I well remember a week of camping out in the

Okefenokee Swamps of South Georgia. Swamp moss was gathered to make a comfortable bed. And then, the pain of sleeping with bugs became very real — an experience to be repeated much too often in later mission trips. My 86 merit badges were a record at that time and proof positive that I was developing the persistence that my entire adult life would demand. There is little doubt that I would have gone into professional work with the Boy Scouts of America had the Lord not called me to the ministry during my second year of college.

With this involvement in scouting came knowledge that came to my service again and again throughout my adult life in missions. In working toward leadership in the Order of the Arrow, I became immersed in the study of American Indian culture. And, I would repeat that study in a dozen other cultures in my lifetime. In earning badges, I learned construction skills, electrician basics, and plumbing. All of these were put to use in construction of churches in remote areas of Mexico and Central America. I learned to do things with what was at hand, and that became the *modus operandi* for mission construction.

But it was the practical knowledge of leadership and the development of my speaking skills that were the most valuable. I learned to stand tall and speak clearly no matter how much my knees shook. I learned that if it was my task to speak, the size and the high rank of the audience made no difference. As I look back over the multitude of letters which praised my public presentations as a teen, I realize how clearly God was preparing me for His work. I was not a "natural talent" so much as I was schooled throughout these years to meet every situation, to speak in spite of all difficulties, to keep myself focused on the goal and to continue as best I could toward the goals before me. Thus,

I did learn that no weakness and no circumstances could keep me from my appointed mission.

Through the Scout program, I entered into my first public speaking. I was an "on fire" promoter of the Scouts. From the local Kiwanis Club to social groups throughout North Georgia, I evangelized about Boy Scouts. The notoriety led to my election to a position on the Youth Temperance Council. I served as the first state president in Georgia. Travel to the Baltimore convention, speeches at the state legislature, and travel throughout the state were a part of my efforts to support alcohol control and educate the youth to the dangers of drinking. All of this brought to my life dedication to principles, an ease in public speaking, and a very practical understanding of the workings of government.

Through the Youth Temperance Council of Georgia, and as the state president, I spoke before the Georgia State Legislature on several occasions concerning the issues of youth and alcohol. More leadership training came from this group as I attended sessions in Boston. Activity in these two organizations made me into a rather well-traveled country boy from the North Georgia mountains. Leadership, organization and public speaking skills grew with each trip, with each speaking engagement.

College was the next step and Emmanuel College in Franklin Springs, Georgia, was an obvious choice. We had always had strong church connections there, Dad had supported the College a great deal through his furniture business, and my sister had attended both high school and college there. In fact, I had enrolled there in the ninth grade. But, just after the term began, I became extremely ill and had to return home for the entire year — listening to the radio and avoiding any physical exertion. It was a year of doctor visits every week and white powder drinks every day. That mixture of powder and water left a memory that still makes me wince.

The move to Emmanuel Bible College in Franklin Springs, Georgia, began a shift in focus from scouting to church ministry. Involvement in ministry and evangelization work with college classmates opened a new road that I would never leave. Whether or not we were effective as preachers in those training days is uncertain, but it was in those sessions that I learned the basics of pioneer ministry and evangelism. The same methods used there were to be applied in Cuba, Mexico, and throughout my ministry.

With the completion of two-year degree in theology, I moved on to a four-year college, Mercer University in Macon, Georgia. Working with Dad at Skelton's Furniture Company in the summers taught me all the rudiments of building and upholstery. Dad could build anything if you could find him a picture of it. We also upholstered and restored of antiques. The work of design and decorating became my responsibility. It was during this time that I realized how much sacrifice my illness and college had extracted from Dad.

The start at Mercer was not encouraging. There were eight of us preparing to leave Gainesville and make our trek to Macon. Dad got his truck and piled in all our luggage. We set out on a crisp fall morning, and by afternoon we saw our luggage scattered all over the highway and fields. The wreck was terrible, but somehow, we all survived. The others continued to Mercer with their patched up belongings, but I returned to Gainesville for 10 days of recovery. My physical limitations bubbled just below the surface and, in my discouragement, I decided I would not go on to Mercer. Mother was not well, and medical expenses were increasing. I announced that it was just too costly for me to continue college. It was a short announcement. Dad was firm and clear. I was to go if he had to sell his business to pay for it. Matter settled. I started packing again for Mercer.

"Casanova" was my name. At least, it had been in high school. Because of my poor health, the doctors felt even riding a school bus was too much. So, I had a new "Touring T-Model" by age 15 and a special permit to drive it. Girls in high school really liked the car, and my social life had improved accordingly. With college, I graduated to a new Chevrolet BelAir, and my social interests began to focus more specifically. It looked more and more like marriage was waiting just around the corner and a certain brunette was clearly a leading candidate.

The University of Georgia offered night classes at an off-campus center in Gainesville, and during the summer before leaving for Mercer, I took a class after work. A sister's friend attended there also. And, that is where the friendship began. I knew who Louise was. She was a relative "thrice removed" as scholars of family history would say. So, I knew her by name but really had no attraction to her. During the summer, I walked her home each evening after class. She lived about two blocks north of us, and it was simply the act of a friend taking care of another. There was no hint of romance, but there was a great deal of conversation about future plans and spiritual commitments. I went off to Mercer in the fall and Louise began a road of difficulty that would lead her to her life's work.

Mercer was not an easy road. The sporadic education of my high school years began to intrude on my academic progress. Quality grades didn't come easy, and sometimes they didn't come at all. My later achievements in areas such as the Spanish language certainly were not evidenced on my college transcript. Other stresses came in the form of theological differences with faculty. Pentecostal theology was basic to me. Mercer is a Baptist school. I was a mountain boy, small in stature, and given to strong opinions. At least once, the confrontation cost me a passing class grade. All faculty do NOT appreciate open debate. But, every failure has a lesson. The lesson in that class: "Learn When to Keep Your Mouth Shut!" Yet, Mercer University was never "out to get me." In spite of confrontations in theology, I received a good education and a great deal of help. Part of my tuition was paid through a ministerial scholarship from the university that I never had to pay back as long as I remained in the ministry.

At Mercer, there were two sides — the good and the bad. In other areas, these same two sides always surfaced. My weekends were spent in pastoring two small churches, speaking at each on alternating weekends. The people in Greston were country folks. I never felt more welcome. Sunday was spent in homes open to me, good food, and loving support. The other weekend was spent in Eastman, Georgia, among a more legalistic group. They were more "up town" and some members kept me well outside their circle of acceptance. One church deacon was particularly concerned about my attending a university to "learn to preach." The pay was small and I found myself having to borrow money just to get gas to get back to Macon on Sunday night. So, as in every situation, the good and the bad were there. I had to enjoy the Greston weekend of food and acceptance enough to last me through the next weekend in Eastman. And, of course, it all made me grow and learn. Whatever the circumstance, my task was to do the job I was called to do. Situations, whether good or bad, are no excuse for poor performance. My responsibilities to both congregations were the same. Eventually this attitude brought acceptance in the Eastman Church, and I developed some very close relationships among the members there also.

During this time, my friend Louise was facing great problems. I had established a friendship with her, and in that year I learned to admire her courage. In that year, Louise was diagnosed with tuberculosis. It was a sad pronouncement to such a young woman. These were the days when TB was a long illness, treated in sanitariums, and beyond the reach of most medicines. She was sent to the north Georgia town of Rome to the state tuberculosis hospital. With friends, I would make the trip to visit her. I learned of her unwavering faith and of her refusal for procedures that she felt were not desirable. But, as she spent days in the hospital, she was in constant prayer. The Lord spoke to her that He would heal her if she would have faith to leave that hospital and go to the mission field. Louise was not given to foolishness, and this was not an easy decision. Her family disapproved. They were frightened of her rebellion against medical advice and of her thoughts of going "clear out of the country." What would happen if she got sick again and was way off where they couldn't help? What if she died in some place that they couldn't even find on a map? It was a courageous woman who rose from the bed and said, "I'm going where God directs me to go."

The insistence of her family to return to the doctor who had originally diagnosed her tuberculosis was not unreasonable. With full faith, Louise made the appointment in Atlanta and heard the doctor say, "You are a remarkably lucky woman. You have come a long way in a short time. You're tuberculosis is arrested. Just be sure you get plenty of rest until you gain your strength back." It was amazing to all, but to us of spiritual faith, it was just a confirming of what the Lord had spoken in her heart. Now, where was the perfect place to begin her missions work? Cuba, of course! It had the proper climate and Louise's dear friend Dorothy McLean was there as a missionary. Dorothy had already invited her to spend time in this island paradise. So, with her parents and sisters in distress, I drove Louise to the airport and sent her to stay with my missionary sister. This remarkable woman exhibited courage to rise up from a bed of sickness, courage to follow her understanding of the Lord's guidance and the courage to resist the family bonds of love that would pull her to their safety. I saw clearly that this was a person who could stand in times of stress and was able to make the difficult decisions needed to follow spiritual commitment.

And still, we were just friends. While I was struggling with college, Louise was struggling with adjustment to a new culture, a new language, and the new experiences of Cuba. My sister Dorothy had gone there four years earlier where she and her husband worked establishing churches and training workers. She was delighted when Louise came to stay and provide friendship from home. And, of course, with Dorothy there and with my interest in all phases of ministry, it was natural that I should go to visit. In 1951, I took the trip to Cuba. It was the shock of a lifetime.

Atlanta was not the major air hub it has become in modern times, but it was no cow pasture either. But, the airport where I landed in Cuba was exactly that — a cow pasture, complete with grazing cattle. The terminal in Atlanta became a castle of the airways compared to that shack at the end of the runway where I unload my luggage. El Cristo — sounds like a really nice place — before you make the 16-mile trip over bumpy roads in a country where you can't even understand the signs on the stores. And, of course, I couldn't read the street signs. I'm not sure there were any. We traveled up to the topmost hill of the area. Such a large home. Why was it so easy to obtain such a fine place? Well, for one thing, it wasn't so fine inside. And, there was that rumor that it was haunted which kept others in the area from wanting to live there. The "haunted" part was never disproved to my satisfaction. I remember it well as a house of unexplained noises and strange spiritual feeling. But, it was the home of my sister and her family, and they made me welcome.

"Oh, Lord. What am I doing here? I wanted to visit with Dorothy, but why would anyone live in such a place as this. This big house with the long porch looks inviting from a distance, but the lizard is frightening. I think I could have handled the encounter with the frog on the light switch of my room, but the tarantula tied to my bed was a bit much. Sure it was a joke executed by my brother-in-law, but it wasn't really funny to me. Couldn't they at least have screens on the windows? I learned to cook outside in Scouts but the idea of charcoal cooking for every meal is really difficult. And, that bread trick! How can anyone break open a loaf of bread and whack it on the side of the table to shake the ants out and then eat it?" Well, that's what I wanted to say to God and I am sure that I did say it in several hastily contrived prayers. Cuba was far beyond my concept of anything. Why would anyone volunteer to live there and put up with the discomforts? I quickly formulated my plan. The first chance at a plane home would be mine. My religious commitment was to preach the gospel. The obvious place was in a growing congregation with a comfortable parsonage. I would preach them into spiritual responsibility, advise them in distress, comfort them in sorrow, perform weddings for their children and bury them at the end of the way. I would pursue truth in the pulpit and would spread the word about missions to the faithful. I would take offerings for those called to work abroad and would pray for them frequently. All of this, I was prepared to do and would certainly begin doing just as soon as I could get out of this place and back in the good old U.S.A. And, then we went to church.

There are times of reason and there are times of emotion. But, there are times when a heart is gripped by something that is neither. A very few times in life, the fortunate of us have an event that makes us know beyond question what we are meant to do. The meaning of our lives — our individual meaning — is made clear. In my first church service among the Cuban people, I had such an encounter. The spirit of the service clutched at my inner being. The entire experience of that service erased all the sights, sounds, and smells that had made me want to find the first plane back to Georgia. I could have stayed in that one church with that one group of people forever. And, I heard the voice of God saying, "Go home, finish your education, and return to minister to these people." In that moment, my heart came to a peace beyond explanation. My place was not at home any longer. Indeed, my home was forever after to be in "regions beyond."

I did return to the "good ole USA" but not with the same goals and the same focus as when I had left. There was still college to complete, but there was an added awareness that I now knew where I was going in life. Well, I at least knew which road I would take. No one could have figured out where that road would lead through the coming years.

Of course, I took up studies at Mercer again. But I also thought about marriage. It just seemed the right time. I had been dating a girl for some time and was quite fond of her. Yet, as I thought of my future in the ministry and my realization that it would be on the mission field, visions of Louise kept coming into my head. I had learned to like her as a friend during that summer of night classes. I had really come to admire her courage and her dedication to the leadership of the Spirit during her sickness. And, I had seen her compassion and adaptability first hand during my visit to Cuba. All the logic of my mind said "Louise." But what about the heart? My heart agreed with my head on this one.

I wrote my proposal of marriage in a letter — and no answer came. No mail. Was it "yes" or was it "no." Louise says she was praying about things but I would have been happier if she had prayed faster. She did finally accept and we began plans for our wedding . The wedding was in Gainesville on August 9, 1952. A lot of family was present and the Rev. B. L. Cox was the minister. Jo Ann Dollar loaned Louise her wedding dress insisting that there was no need for a new one when that one had been used only once and that just a year or so earlier. The wedding was a celebration except for one of the guests who shed tears as the ceremony began. It was the girl whom I had been seriously dating until Louise and I decided to marry. Why was she there? She had met Louise and myself in a department store in town, and Louise invited her. There are things about women that I never expect to understand!

Louise and I returned to Macon where we both enrolled in Mercer University for the following year. I pastored churches, did upholstery on the side, and she worked in a CPA's office. Having a squeaky tight budget, we saved by sharing rent on a two-bedroom apartment with Bob and Jo Ann Dollar. Bob pastored a small Baptist church in the area and later became Vice-President of Day's Inns. I pastored a Pentecostal church and later became a missionary. We split the rent and shared the kitchen. Whichever of us got an offering for the weekend services bought groceries. It was a tough year but one of wonderful memories.

The events of college life do not always mirror future achievement. I struggled but kept up, except for my Spanish class. Some things you work at and are happy to survive. The "D" in Spanish was survival. And yet, in my later life I made use of Spanish more than any of my other college studies. I later became totally at home in the language for personal conversation, sermons, or interpreting for others. [In reality, his Latin coworkers consider Hugh Skelton one of the best non-native speakers of Spanish.] I just didn't learn it at Mercer. It was in Cuba where I filled pages with written work, spent hours in study, and conversed constantly with the people that I mastered the language.

Oh, yes. There was another major even during that year at Mercer. I graduated with a degree in Theology and a minor in Education. But that was nothing! Louise was pregnant. Our son, Hugh Allen Skelton, made his appearance in March of 1954. We were making plans to go to work as missionaries in Cuba sometime within the next year. I continued pastoring a small church in the area until it became time to start visiting other churches to gather support for our mission plans.

I approached our church leaders about establishing our first real missionary outreach sponsored by the Congregational Holiness Church. They were not opposed. They just had no funds and no prospects of any for such a project. They gave me their permission to raise funds and their blessings, but no monthly check. I began the trek through Georgia, Alabama, Virginia and the Carolinas seeking contributions from tiny poor churches. It was not always an "open door" that we found. Louise and I, with the baby, drove hundreds of miles. There were time when we found the church that invited us had forgotten, and the doors were not even open for service. One cold night in Alabama, I had to turn from the closed locked church and call my old friend, Rev. Alvin Crews, with a plea for a place to stay the evening. And, the response was generous. He insisted that at any time in the future we were in that area we should just come to their home and not even suggest that the local church provide us a place to stay. We were "family" at that home. So, for every church like the one in South Carolina where we drove hundreds of miles to face a closed church, there sprung up "mothers and fathers" in the church who loved us and cared for us with every effort they could make. We always have the choice of seeing either the opposition or the assistance. The love and support from kind country folks far outweighed any neglect we felt from those who did not respond.

Cuba bound! February, 1955. Just gather up all our goods in a tiny trailer. Put Allen and Louise in the car and head for the docks in Key West, Florida. We had a goal in life. We were pioneering new church work in Cuba for the Congregational Holiness Church which had never had an established missions work before. There were friends who helped, who advised, who supported. But, we really were going into uncharted waters with neither a tradition nor experience in the area of pioneer missions. We were rather young and felt an exciting "call to the mission field." Language was no worry. After all, I had taken Spanish at Mercer and knew a few words. And, though now I would consider it a truly short trip, it was the farthest and longest trip this North Georgia preacher could imagine.

Leaving mother in her sickness had been one of my greatest difficulties. Her wave of good-bye from the hospital doorway still lives clear in my memory. I was correct in that I would not see her again in this lifetime. We were in Cuba only six months before making a rapid return for her funeral. Leaving Dad alone was painful. The son who could have helped him in his business and in his personal pain was to be far away. The large Georgia family that had always been part of our lives was left for a country of strangers. My family of three, Louise, Allen and I, were headed for an island — physically and socially. We were leaving close family members and supportive friends for the unfamiliar. But our dreams pressed us southward and our spirits bubbled hope and delight in the midst of the sadness.

The sunshine of Key West and the beautiful Caribbean water are stuff of dream vacations. And, of course, writers such as Ernest Hemingway and the socially prominent had made that cruise over to Cuba — that short 90-mile boat ride — a famed journey. How long was that boat ride with 125 passengers on board that late winter day? It was an eternity! In all my crossings to Cuba, never was there such a rough ride. The entire boat road on waves of vomit from seasick passengers. All three of us contributed our share.   At last, the Havana harbor area appeared. And with it, came the calmest seas one can ever experience.   It was as though the storm melted into nothingness. We gathered our stomachs and our goods and drove off the boat onto the island of Cuba. It was 1952. We were headed for a new life, and Cuba was not far from an even rockier road than we were.

Six years later, I looked down on the island of Cuba and watched it slide from view in an airplane window. My narrow escape from arrest and time in Castro's prison produced a relief that masked the sadness felt from leaving a place Louise and I had loved. It was a "first child" of our ministry and there would never be another like it. But, my need of that moment was to be at home, to care for the health of my wife, to nurture my small son, and to recover from the immense physical and mental stress of the years of war and violence. It was in exhaustion, the exhaustion of a task completed, that I looked down on the receding Cuba and looked forward toward the mountains of home.

7

After Cuba

Louise had been spared the stress of the last Cuban days, but that wasn't because she was vacationing in the states. The blood loss that she saw during those times was her own. Hemorrhaging began late one night. A call to the doctor for emergency help brought the news: "She can be dead in two minutes. It is beyond our help for her in Santiago. You must get her to the United States."

I began my frantic run for help. Red Cross — no help, US Embassy — can't do anything; US Naval Base at Guantanamo — Sorry! A nightmare — an absolute nightmare for a young husband with a small son and no one to turn to. Surely it was the power of prayer being put forth by our Cuban friends that saved her life. They prayed in a human prayer chain during that night and those prayers gave me strength to press on and believe we could make it.

With the hemorrhaging slowed, I searched frantically to get a plane flight to the states. Two tickets for Louse — she could not sit up — and one for me. We headed for Miami on commercial wings and more than one person's prayers. The storm that hit us was as bad as I have encountered in three million miles of flying since. Late arrival in Miami — missed flight to Atlanta. Nothing was going right. It was spiritually dark and lonely in the Miami airport awaiting another flight with my dying wife in a wheel chair beside me. The memory still makes my stomach weak.

But, darkness precedes dawn and the good news was awaiting. A return to her regular physician in Atlanta led to surgery and the removal of a lobe of her lung. In it, they found the tubercular germs totally contained. There would be no spread and the prognosis was that she would feel better and be healthier than she had ever been in her life. It was to be so. Though a weakness from lower lung capacity lasted a lifetime, Louise was a stronger healthier person in the years to come. Some time of recovery was needed so she and Allen went to to stay with her mother in North Georgia where Allen enrolled in school. I returned to Cuba to vacate the house and prepare the churches for the uncertain days ahead of them.

RETURN TO MISSIONS

December of 1961 marked my final trip from Cuba. It was good to be home and hear the silence — no shell firings, no bombs exploding, no screams of fear and pain. People in North Georgia walked the streets without a constant fear on their faces. They did not wonder if their family members had been arrested while they were buying groceries. It was a markedly different world. So, why didn't we stay in the nest of the family that cared for us, a place where Allen was adjusting to school life? The call of our lives was to missions and our inner beings were not satisfied with the norm. The people of Cuba had become our people. We moved to Tampa to work with those who were coming from Cuba in any way they could.

My sister, Dorothy, was again our point of direction. She was teaching at a high school in Tampa, Florida, and the Cuban refugees were there in abundance. With her as a contact point, I gathered up Louise and Allen for a pastorate with the Emmanuel Christian Assembly there. It was a bi-lingual Pentecostal church and, a job — not a position but a JOB. Holding three services a week in Spanish and three each week in English was more than full-time work. For over a year, we worked there, bought a small house and thought we were settled for a few years. Until, I went traveling with Rev. Sixto Lopez.

My heart yearned for the foreign fields of ministry. Mexico or Venezuela? When opportunity came to take a survey of missions needs in Mexico with a former Cuban missionary, I was ready to go. Sixto and I traveled throughout Mexico visiting small villages as well as large cities, including Mexico City. Even as we entered the country, the spiritual voice of God let me know that this was where I would return to mission work. On our return home, I told Louise and her response was the usual support of whatever the Lord directed. It was only once of many times that I knew I had married the right woman — one who was constant in her response to the call of the work. Many would have said "Enough. I don't want to leave our little home — the first one that is really ours. What about Allen and his school?" We were moving to South Texas to begin work in Mexico. It was simple, and it was not a struggle. Even the business matters fell into place.

"Lord, I need to sell this house." I walked from that prayer to my front yard and began conversing with a neighbor. "If you know anyone wanting to buy a house, we are selling this one?"

"How much?" and a response from me led to "Let's go get the paper work done now." The house sale was completed within 30 minutes of my prayer.

MEXICO

Pharr, McAllen, hospitals, car wrecks, stonings, our largest and most successful missions effort — this is the Mexican story for us. As a family, we moved to Pharr, Texas, for a few months until we found a home in McAllen, Texas, for our next 10 years. There we would begin our ministry in Mexico, see it grow to over 230 churches, train others interested in missions and see our son through his youth. Mexico is a story of people — people and cooperation — people and love.

"Whom may I say is calling upon her?" asked Floradelle Baldwin. I didn't know Floradelle at the time but thought it an oddly formal response to my effort to contact an old college friend, June Carter. We had been at Emmanuel together, and I knew that June would be a great help with starting a Mexican work. She was from a true missions family with a father who was a leader of ministers and a sister on the mission field in India. June had been in the Rio Grande Valley for several years now in Bible School work. I was anxious to see her but didn't know about her co-worker — Ms. Baldwin of the formal questioning. As it turned out, both ladies were just great folks to be with and to work with. Through them and a Mexican minister I had met in Reynosa, Mexico, we began our church work in Mexico.

The laws of Mexico were tough. They prohibited any foreign establishment of religious works and forbade services in the "open air". The Beltran family of Reynosa were the key to our new efforts. They lived very near the US/Mexico border. With a tarp over their patio area, we could start Sunday School services. My friend, Rev. Guevarra, introduced me to a young Mexican Bible School student named Jose Rubio. Jose worked with Louise to canvass the neighborhood and set up our first Sunday School on October 13, 1963. They had 63 attending — mostly women and children. That would set our format for beginning works in Mexico. Sunday School came first with children and sometimes mothers attending. Later evening services would develop which the men would attend.

Another precept of our missions work was national leadership. We were able to walk out of Cuba and leave churches that would survive 40+ years of persecution, poverty, and Communist rule. As Cuba gradually opened to American visitors in the late 1990's, we found a core of our work and gospel teachings still alive. Contact through intricate sources had continued through the years but the stability and the continuance of the work was due to durable native leadership. The missionary's job is to work himself or herself out of a job! Of foremost concern is to make every Christian effort the effort of those living in the area. Americans have no special place with God that makes them always wiser and always more influential. No outsider of any community can understand and do more than a leader within that community. We have always been blessed to find leadership from within and to work with that leadership as partners. There can be no greater proof of this than Rev. Jose Rubio.

Jose was introduced as a young Bible school student. He helped pioneer our first church, canvassed neighborhoods, helped with Sunday Schools, preached sermons, met with legal and political authorities, pastored churches, began radio ministries, led conferences, and held the hand of struggling missionaries along the way. The story of Mexico is a story of Jose. After church work was in progress near the border, we moved to Central Mexico and the home area of Jose. It was in Morelia that we would establish our first Bible School. Jose served in every capacity including chief contractor of churches and as pastor of our headquarters church in Reynosa. He served as leader of the national conference, later established a successful radio ministry reaching throughout Central America, and directed a massive Bible distribution ministry among Latin Americans. With his wife, Mary, and their three children, the work has been a family affair. They are not only the cornerstone of the Mexican church effort but are the finest examples of what committed Christians can do in evangelizing their own people.

From Jose's friendship, we acquired other great Mexican national workers. He had a close relative who had begun Christian ministry in Central Mexico with his message of the Gospel brought from the work fields of North Texas. As we assisted, villages began to open to gospel teaching. With the help of Jose Arroyo and his brother Joaquin, we survived travel through mountain villages, opposition to foreigners, and even an episode of stoning as we worked to establish churches. The official organizing of the Congregational Holiness Church in Mexico was done during a visit of Bishop Terry Crews and Rev. B. A. Skelton in the Taraascan Indian town of Cueneo, Mexico, near the Morelia home of the Arroyo family. From this beginning, our first Bible School was built in Morelia, Michoacan, Mexico. The work there was an example of family evangelization. Brothers brought brothers and family members gathered in other family. Native evangelism took root, and the heroes were those Mexican brothers and sisters who sacrificed of their lives for the growth of the church.

The stories of Mexican heroes could fill a book in themselves. Rev. Jose Arroyo had suffered persecution for his gospel teaching in a time and land where Protestant religion was not accepted. He and his brother were beaten and left for dead in one village. In another, he was spiritually awakened in the middle of the night and felt he should leave immediately. He and his co-worker left before the sunrise greeted a mob of over 200 persons seeking to kill them. I, myself, was with him in a village just to discuss the beginning of a church mission when a large crowd began to gather. We left the village among a barrage of stones flung at us from every side. However, the result was a church of over 300 attendees. Where there is most opposition to be faced, there is often the most potential for success.

The Mexico church work eventually stretched from Reynosa on the US border to the jungles of Chiapas and the border of Guatemala with the churches operating under a totally Mexican leadership. There are churches in big cities and in tiny "barrios". Lampacitos is a good view of the typical village. Actually, Lampacitos was more of an area than a village. It sits in the high dusty desert-like area of the northern border. The poorest of families invited us in to have services. They moved their own living area into one room to give a vacant front room for the church. In the heat, we would often string a tarp outside for services and preach through the noise of pigs and the wandering of chickens through the service, but they never outnumbered the interested people. In a barren area not even called a village, a church of over 600 grew. Today a church building has been given to the people in honor of my younger brother Joe who died accidentally at the age of 33.

Guadalupe de la Joya was far from the beaten track. In "the middle of no where," one wonders how we ever arrived over the miles of potholes and mud to find such a place. From the village leadership, Anacleto and Lucia Pena came forth as pastors. They eventually pastored our headquarters church in Reynosa and raised an unbelievable family of educated talented children — all successful in their professions and supporters of evangelical gospel work.

And, of course, there was adventure along the way — and laughter. Nights in hospitals were not the fun parts. My physical weakness was a constant battle. I remember large city hospitals, small town doctor's offices, and nights in places such as Concepcion del Oro with just a clinic bed. The Latin hospital usually meant bring your own linens, have a friend bring you food, the possibility of a few flies and other creatures through poorly maintained screens, no air conditioning and even a lack of heat when needed. But, doctors were generally competent and concerned. I made my visits as short as possible, and always prayed again that the Lord would heal me of the infirmities of flesh that disrupted my travels. But, He never agreed with me on that subject. I had to learn to agree with Him and accept whatever came my way.

The laughter usually had more to do with custom differences and American visitors. Many church groups came to visit among the Latin works and that meant some adaptation. The main conference in Central Mexico was a time of celebration and the U.S. contingency was always welcome. It was a good time to worship together and to share visions of future growth of the church work. But, for this one, I thought that some toilet facility might be in order. Most Americans are just not comfortable with heading out to the goat pen without even a semblance of an outhouse. And, of course, the local leaders understood my request of "improved facilities" for our visitors. At least, I thought they understood. We arrived for conference time completely prepared for a day of preaching, eating, and discussing church plans. I quickly excused myself to check on the "Outhouse Project" and was told all was finished. A quick escort to the area revealed nicely erected panels awaiting any calls of natures. The clean look and smell of new wooden facilities was a real work of art. But, why the open air space at the bottom? Why were the side panels 2 1/2 foot off the ground? Somehow the modesty focus was missed when the area from panel to ground was left open. Of course, they were "airy" and "refreshing."

The encounters in cultural gaps and dealing with a different way of life called for constant adjustment of ideas and attitudes. What do you do when a large angry bull decides to stand across the road in front of your Volkswagon Beetle? Well, you yell a lot — no movement. You pray some — not a spiritually responsive bull! You do not get out of the car. Ahh! Of course. You take a floppy hat and wave it out the car window until the bull moves. Why did it take so long to think of that?

And, that same flapper of hats, Rev. Johnnie Roberts, was the source of my greatest fright in Mexico. He and Rev. Gerald Sanders were with me in the city. Mexico City — the famed sinking capital built on swamp land replete with stagnant air, millions of people, and drivers that cannot be imagined. The memory of a night at the Plaza de Belles Artes is of a speeding car. It hit both of the other men and grazed the pants on my legs. Rev. Roberts flew high in the air; Rev. Sanders was thrown several yards down the street. In a dark street, alone with what appeared to be two dead men, I began to pray. From somewhere came the prayer to "raise these men up." And, they began to stir. Both men rose together, apparently unhurt. The arriving policemen required us to be checked out at the hospital where absolutely no injuries were found. Two men (one over six-foot tall and the other over 200 lbs.) had been thrown several feet and suffered no injury at all. To me, it was a miracle — one of the many that kept my faith always looking forward. After all, I did "live on the edge of a miracle."

MTC: VISION — TRAINING — ACTION

We lived in McAllen, Texas, and traveled often over the nine miles to the Mexican border. I really believe that I could have built my own bridge for the cost of the toll we paid to cross that border so many times. One of our goals other than evangelization in Mexico was the training of young workers in missions. There is often a glorified idea of missions work that attracts people, and when they hit the hard realities, such visions fade. The Missionary Training Center was established to give a short-term missions experience and training to those with an interest. It served to help people interested in missions work make quality decisions about their service in evangelism.

It was summertime and there was work to be done! Clean the buildings, buy new supplies, and get ready for two weeks of total action. "Vision-Training-Action." That was the motto of the training center and adding several dozen teens to the mix certainly got the "action" part into it. Students ranged from teens to retirement age, but most were in late high school or early college. They were searching and making decisions for their lives. Two weeks of classroom work in McAllen was designed to teach about cultural differences, evangelism and some survival skills. It also did a lot to teach adaptation to group living. But, there was never enough teaching to cover the need. When the two weeks of travel into Mexico began, the true self surfaced in each of us.

This was the work that infused us with vision for the future. It tired the body but energized the spirit. Despite long trips, sleeping on church benches, stomach sickness and whatever else came, the MTC students always gave it all they had. Of over 350 students in ten years, 135 of them became firmly involved in missions work. And others found the equally important truth that they were supporters of foreign work but not the "called." It was a time of discovery — about themselves and about evangelism.

Nothing symbolizes those summer sessions like the buses involved. The groups spent hot hours on old school buses with stops on the side of the road to fix sandwiches and Kool-Aid. Few trips were made without praying the bus through at least one episode. Night travel was a total "no no" in Mexico. And, yet we were forced into crossing the last mountains into Mexico City with darkness at hand. The popping under the bus began about two hours out of town. There was no visible problem — just the noise. Students formed a prayer spot in the back of the bus and took turns praying as we traveled. Daylight revealed back wheels that were almost off the bus due to improper wear on the lug bolts. The great butane experiment was another bus. It ran fine if you weren't afraid of explosions. Students sat on hard school bus seats and on one trip even an ice chest was the permanent seat of one passenger.

Much of the Latin American expansion came from students at these sessions. Rev. Randall Chester was our first student and later opened the work in Costa Rica. Rev. L. M. Reese and his wife Beverly spent a summer at the Center and went on to pioneer work in Brazil. Supporters from Georgia, such as the Garvice Elliot family, J. D. Sosebee, Johnnie Roberts and Wes Barlow came to help out and drive the bus. Missionaries such as June Carter and Rev. Willard Harmon volunteered their expertise to teach and work with the students. Everything from teaching to cooking was done by dedicated volunteers. And, we learned to live and worship and give as one. It was a decade of foundation for mission work in the denomination.

HARD TIMES AND CHANGES

"Allen's hurt. We have to get home." Louise's voice shook and fear that had never come from travel situations was in her eyes. The call had come from McAllen and had finally reached us in Mexico City. Because we had changed hotel plans at the last minute, it had taken days to reach us. Those with us understood that the trip would have to be cut short. We had to get back.

It was a motorcycle accident. Allen was with Edward and Vivian Smith and their two boys. The Smiths had moved out to McAllen some months before to take up missions work with us. Smitty had retired from the Army, and they left their Alabama home to start a new ministry in Texas. Their two boys were perfect companions for Allen so he was staying with them while we were away. On a dusty south Texas afternoon, the boys had pulled out of an orange grove trail into the side of a car. Allen was hospitalized with a hairline fracture in his neck and a fractured ankle. Jerry, the Smith's son, was rushed to the Harlingen, Texas, hospital with even worse injuries.

Things were dim and dark as we left Mexico City to get home, and we found no cooperation of circumstances in our journey. The drive over the mountains ended abruptly with a broken water pump. Eight hours of waiting for help with a frantic mother and fear in my own heart was not easy. The problems necessitated a return to Mexico City, another night of waiting and then the long two-day journey home. And in those worst of times, it was friends who always stood by and took care. They were dependable. The "family" of workers and friends in McAllen spread out to stay at Allen's bedside and with the Smith family around the clock. Others stayed by the phone to contact us. Phone calls and prayers traveled from Texas to Georgia and across the country. We came home to find our son hospitalized but stable and well. We found our friends Vivian and Smitty facing the worst moments of their lives.

Their son's situation was critical. The ambulance driver who picked him and his broken skull up from the highway insisted that it was the worst case he had ever seen that survived. The Smiths spent torturous days in south Texas military hospitals and more months back in Alabama before Jerry could speak or respond. The accident happened in early October, and it would be Thanksgiving before they left his bedside for even an hour. But, he did recover. The tall handsome sixteen-year-old would never walk without a limp and would suffer the consequences of the stress on his brain forever. But, he did smile again, he did find a career, and his recovery still stirs our spirits with wonder at the reliability of God in times of need.

For the Smith family, the event marked a return to Alabama and a pastoral ministry there. For our family, the mark of movement was not so clearly drawn, but it was from that time that our return to the southeast began to take shape. It was not that Allen was not as well as ever. Nor was it the fact that those stormy years of the teens brought more than the usual parental stress. Decreasing physical strength forced me to furlough in Georgia for nine months. We returned to the work in McAllen where Allen completed high school. But, he then chose to move to North Georgia to live with his grandmother and decide his own future.

It was evident that our work was changing in nature. The Mexican Conference was successfully operating under local leadership, and there was need for leadership in missions on a denominational level. The work had begun to spread throughout Central America so Louise and I packed our bags again, sold the house, and journeyed back to Georgia. This time, it was to become Superintendent of World Missions at church headquarters in Griffin, Georgia.

8

Latin American Expansion

COSTA RICA — 1966

Costa Rica has what are probably the most modern hospital facilities of the Central American countries. So, of course, I never stayed in one of them. I did, however, spend time in an "hourly rental" motel and had a true ride "on the rails." We planned the trip that took us over a ravine with our car tires balancing on railroad tracks. There was no other way to get to our village church service. The stay at a less than reputable hotel was an accident of financial need and ignorance of the area. Louise, my sister Dorothy, and Randall Chester and I made a trip down to plan future evangelism in the country. We were traveling cheap and managed to see all aspects of the area.

Located centrally in the Central American chain, Costa Rica is an oasis of beauty. Renowned for government stability and an educated populace, it was a perfect starting point for church growth. This "little Switzerland of the Americas" boasts high mountains, coffee plantations and active volcanoes. And in almost equal proportion are the low jungles, white beaches and banana plantations. The people take pride in their clean house and shrubbery enhanced yards. The finely painted ox carts are symbolic of their love of beauty. Located in the midst of countries undergoing civil war, the military of Costa Rica takes back seat numerically and financially to their educational programs. Their neutrality is transgressed only by multitudes of mosquitoes and insects in the lowlands. And, it has one of the finest language schools in all of Latin America — the focus of Rev. Chester's interest at that time.

From that first trip, Randall laid plans to return and begin work there. He and his wife Sharon were to spend many years working within the country. The effort there resulted in over 30 churches and 3000 members. Though San Jose is the modern capital, the strength of the church was in the coffee strewn mountain towns such as Turrialba. Modern living and an upscale life style mark the country where illiteracy is almost unknown. Thus, it was that Rev. Roy Wellborn and I spent three embarrassing days wearing the same clothes — in a steamy jungle. The airline had lost our clothes, and we had no time to wait for suitcases. Our commitments were set so we sweated our way through the meetings. The one white shirt that Rev. Wellborn wore came out of that jungle in a fine beige tone. We had no laundry after that trip; it all went directly to the trash.

HONDURAS — 1967

"Señor, Matute?" At last, I was meeting the man recommended to help us establish churches in Honduras. It was a three-plane trip — a four-motor job to San Pedro Sula followed by a two-motor plane to La Ceiba and then a tiny piper cub to the mountain area where we had set our meeting. But, it was not Señor Matute who greeted me. The cow pasture airstrip reminded me of Cuba and so did the four armed soldiers coming toward me. Fearfully, I followed and conversed with them. Slowly, I realized that I was being giving some sort of VIP treatment and not prisoner-of-war questions. Treading carefully, linguistically as well as physically, I toured the place. Photos — they wanted me to take more photos. Oh yes, whatever they wanted. The cock fight — oh let me get pictures of that! But my mind wondered continually, "Why am I watching a cock fight? Why am I taking photos? Who do they think I am?" And most of all, what if they find out I'm not the guest they expected. I was aware that their weapons were fully loaded and in place.

"¿Señor Skelton?" It was definitely a question from the tall Honduranian who appeared at last.

"Ah, yes. You must be Señor Matute," I responded with great relief. Excusing myself with great politeness, I left the soldiers with a smile and a few last photos. And, I never mentioned that I was not the photographer from Life Magazine they had been expecting. It had taken a great deal of time and silent listening to comprehend the mix up, and I certainly wasn't telling four machine guns that I had been shown their great hospitality by mistake. The land of Honduras has proved itself to be a land of great miracles — and my visit there may have started with a small miracle of safety.

Rain, mountains, and poverty mark the Honduranian countryside. But, the people respond to the gospel and to friendship as none other. Sacrifice is a way of life and hardship is faced with courage. Rev. Ray Alvarado and his wife Nona Jo gave years of their lives to directing the church development there. The harvest was over 345 churches, a Bible School and a strong national leadership under a lively and talented minister, Rev. Tito Rodriguez. The Alvaradoes left the country some years later due to her health problems. Their adopted son, Paco, became a US citizen and has entered ministerial training as a second-generation missionary. Nona Jo lived only a few years after leaving Honduras suffering from diabetically caused blindness.

The first church in Honduras was built from mud and sticks in Choloma. The people had no money but they willingly worked with what was at hand. And in such churches, miraculous events are reported with astonishing frequency. I can only repeat the stories of the sick healed and the dead raised. Among those miracles reported is a bridge washed out by one of the floods so frequent in the area. Concerned about the needs of his congregation there, the local pastor drove to see how he could help. His car was immediately surrounded by excited people in the center of the village. "How did you get here? How did you cross the river gorge?"

"I drove as before," he insisted.

"Imposible, Señor! Imposible"

The bridge had been washed away in the storm. The ravine could not be crossed. To prove his point, the pastor led them back to the bridge — and found a broken bridge and a raging river below. Such stories are common to the Honduras church. And why should they not be? Of all of the countries I have ever visited, none pray as these people do. They can pray for hours. The church has gone forward in the hands of the women of the country who are filled with faith and good works. What little they have in goods and finance seems constantly multiplied to meet the needs. The poverty of Honduras is in direct contrast to the wealth of faith.

BRAZIL — 1972

Rev. Willard Harmon invited us to visit him and his mission work in Manaus, Brazil. He was located on the

Black River in the heart of the Brazilian jungle. There were no roads. Boat travel (or plane) was the only way in or out. Why build roads when the jungle would simply cover them over within 3-6 months? Housing was scarce — almost impossible. But, it was here that L. M. and Beverly Reese would live and begin their family. It was our first foreign work that was not Spanish speaking. At L.M.'s funeral following a plane crash in 1995, I proudly spoke of him as "a servant of God." Never in my work have I seen a family that worked any harder, studied more diligently, or suffered greater deprivation during their tenure of missionary work. The living conditions were atrocious — and never did they complain.

The city of Manaus was the one-time crown jewel of the Amazon valley. It was the center of the rubber kingdom in the early 1900's and still boasts a fine opera house that is the pride of the area. Where once lords and ladies of wealth lived in servant-laden households, today's people live in a steamy bug infested harbor area. The harbor of Manaus is still the largest floating harbor in the world though it is located 1500 miles inland. The Amazon River is the greatest of the world's river highways. And, the once proud city bears all the dangers and trash of a riverfront city.

It was in Brazil that I encountered the miracles and mice. Actually, they were rats. We stayed in the home of a church family in Belen for the days of the conference. I had not counted on a rat in my bed, but there one appeared for two successive nights. Rev. Milton Martin who was traveling with me experienced no such problem. How could it be that I was so lucky! Yet, as always, the success of the services and the progress of the church work made such "inconveniences" seem minor.

A more startling occurrence was the miracle of our trip. Our schedule indicated we were to visit the city of Manacapuru the very end of the only road out of Manaus. Transportation was needed, but the only car available belonged to one of our church members who had lost his eyesight. No problem! At the end of the evening service in Manaus, Rev. Martin called the owner of the car to come forward for prayer. The healing was truly miraculous. With restored sight, the man appeared promptly the next day and drove us down the jungle road to our destination.

When the Reese family left Brazil to take leadership as Missions Superintendent for the general church, they left mission works scattered over a thousand miles up and down the riverways. And in keeping with the pattern, the works have continued to grow and prosper under native leadership.

For true adventure, nothing beats an Amazon taxi ride. Crowded boats provide small deck space for passengers. Take your own hammock and stretch it in the open air. Be careful where you step lest you find yourself in someone else's bedroom. Carry plenty of supplies and be prepared to cook all meals on a community cooker filled with charcoal somewhere near the rear of the boat. Don't drag your feet in the water — it is the land of the piranha. And, be friendly. You will be close neighbors with a lot of strangers for the entire trip if you don't make them your friends.

As a Spanish-speaker in a land where Portuguese is spoken, I found communication difficult. I could understand native speech fairly well, but the French intonation found in Portuguese has always made speaking the language very difficult. But the barriers to evangelism in Brazil go beyond the language problem. The Brazilian jungle is so vast and so thick that totally unreached villages and tribes have never seen or heard the gospel message in any form. This physical isolation of communities makes Brazil a fertile field for evangelism requiring many years of commitment and labor.

GUATEMALA — 1974

Earthquakes and rebel soldiers. High mountains, travel by horseback, and cold cold weather. The church work in Guatemala centered in the mountains where summer days seldom saw warmth enough to shed one's long sleeves. The government situation is always fragile and always unstable. But, there are few restrictions on evangelistic work and a people hungry for spiritual teaching. From the flight into Guatemala City, a four and a half hour ride into the mountains to Quetzaltenango is needed to find the work begun with Rev. James Remick and his family. That ride is often by bus with frequent stops for searches by armed soldiers — sometimes national troops, sometimes rebel groups.

A major quake had left the nation in shambles. I arrived three days after and found railroad tracks twisted over the earth like giant snakes, trees split into halves, and buildings pulverized. Stories of family loss were common. One lady saw the earth open and swallow the house with her children inside before closing over them. Superintendent Arnoldo Rivera lost his entire family in the quake. And, the churches were full. In times of distress, people move to God and the church for both spiritual comfort and physical resources, and it is the duty of Christians to respond to those needs. In Guatemala, we joined the native leaders to provide food, to rebuild, and to supply the needs of all we could reach. This faithfulness to share and to serve resulted in rapid growth of the evangelism effort. Devastated by the power of destructive forces, Guatemalans seek and experience God in the details of their daily lives, and the churches of this country are marked by the power of God at work.

Power meets power and that means danger. The travel is dangerous on mountain pathways by horseback to meet in indigenous Indian villages of varying dialects. The cities are crime filled. I struggled for an eternity in a matter of seconds with a thief's hand caught in my pants pocket. Like the story of the monkey with his hand in a jar of coins, I refused to let go his wrist until he turned loose of the money. Then, I was glad to release his hand and let him run. The unstable government and the harshness of life make everyone a target for thieves — but foreigners are a clear financial target. Companies employing American workers provide protected housing and transport as part of the employee package. Company executives are provided with personal bodyguards.

And, yet the people are generally kind and giving in nature. They suffer the stresses of their lives and their economic uncertainty with strength. The Indian countenance is not revealing nor given to emotional outbursts. They just shoulder the load as they have carried their firewood and their other burdens over the years. They do not run rapidly forward but walk steadily up the chosen path. They will reach their destiny in Christ.

NICARAGUA — 1988

"Señor. All the hospitals are closed. They are on strike. We can get you to the military hospital, but you must do as I say. I will tell them you are my father." It seemed a reasonable plan. I had been violently ill for hours and can remember no time when I felt nearer death. A neighbor came with his Volkswagen and drove. Our native minister helped me into the vehicle, and the nurse rode beside me in the back seat. I was in no shape to argue and yet something did not seem right. As I floated in and out of consciousness, I realized that this was a totally daring effort to fool military guards with guns. It was a good story — but the lovely nurse was so black and I was so white!

But it did work. She knew her medicine, and she knew how to get things done. As we approached the sentry gate, she pulled the blanket high around me and told me to sit with my face low between my knees. It wasn't hard to do since I was sick enough to roll into a ball and die. At her word, "It is my father," we were allowed to pass.

The sickness had a known source this time. In our plans to visit churches in the Nicaraguan countryside, we had acted foolishly. We had rented a car and set out without food and without water. It was never to be done and though our destination and planned meals were but a few hours away, the car breakdown left us sitting in 110 degree heat the entire day without liquids. Dehydration had set in by the time an evening bus came by and gave us transport back to the city. I made it through the planned church service and then collapsed. But, now I was at the hospital with IV's of glucose flowing into each arm, and, at 4:00 a.m., they came for my bed. The Nicaraguans were not being cruel. They were just in the midst of another of the crippling strikes associated with revolutionary times. All hospitals were closed except for the military and worse needs than mine had to be taken care of. How much of my life has been spent in the midst of political rebellion and revolutions? I have seen rebel soldiers with machine guns in almost every country except for Costa Rica. And though some of these countries are in continued turmoil, most are not. It is just that the timing of my life and of my work among very peaceful people seems to coincide with times of danger and upheaval.

As dawn broke in Managua, we drove back through the streets in the Volkswagen. The wonderful nurse held one bottle of glucose as we traveled while our pastor held the other. They carried me into the house and hung the bottles on a curtain rod to continue their drip as I rested. Amazingly, I arose by service time and was able to attend the duties of moderator for the conference.

The Sandanistas and Contras in conflict had hindered any American visit to the church work in the country for some time. It was the Costa Rican church that had pioneered the missionary effort in the war torn country. Rev. Zacarias Campos took the message home to Nicaragua and began work that cut its teeth on revolution and ministered through gun battles and worldwide political discord. Nicaragua is a landmark in our missionary effort as it is the first true second-generation work. It resulted from mission work in Costa Rica, which took upon itself the Gospel imperative to spread the evangelical news.

As the work in Honduras is marked by the efforts of the women, the work of Nicaragua is marked by its ministry to children. The capital city of Managua is as strange as any to be seen. After devastation by an earthquake, the center of the city was never rebuilt. One travels through city suburbs and then reaches a core of nothingness — flat nothingness. Across that flattened area, the city edges start up again. To me, it symbolizes the country itself. The people go on with their everyday lives, but something is missing. The long days of revolution and the tragedy of earthquakes show as lines of concern on their faces. It is as though the center of their lives has been taken, and they survive on the edges. It is no wonder that their focus is on the generations of the future. The church work runs a large active day school and education is a major concern. Maybe someone will teach their children peace, and I pray, Lord, it will be us — the brotherhood and sisterhood of Christianity — that does the job.

EL SALVADOR — August, 1988

North of Nicaragua is the more coastal and tiny country of El Salvador. It has only a Pacific Coast rather than the dual coast of other Central American countries, and it has but one major city — the capital, San Salvador. Our church effort began there as the result of meeting with an independent church minister, Rev. Bernadino Mena. After the establishing of strong church work in several countries, it has become fairly common to have independent pastors approach us to join our organized conferences. I have no doubt that this is a result of our insistence on local leadership and native governance. Other nationalities have their own cultural ways and often they do not fit the expectation of the American church. However, they are intelligent people, and they are totally capable of growing and directing their own destinies as churches.   We are equipped to assist and to teach. Christianity is about sharing what God has given us. I find among my Latin brothers, ministers who teach me truths of the Gospel.   I see in them lessons of patience and of endurance. For all we have given, we have received many times over.

With church work established in Guatemala, Honduras and Nicaragua, the El Salvador area was a natural area for church expansion. It was also a natural area for revolutionary expansion. So, again we met with men who lived within the area and supported their efforts to combat war and poverty to establish churches. The missions were well underway before I as an American was permitted to visit the country. And, the last two times I have made effort to visit, my American citizenship caused me to be put on the plane through to Costa Rica. Our co-worker with Mexican citizenship, Jose Rubio was allowed to stay a few days to confer with the superintendent of our work. Of course, I wasn't too bothered. Jose's report of gun battles and bomb explosions left me with no envy. And, he said that sleeping under the bed was really not comfortable.

The church leadership has passed from father to son and Rev. Mena provides great leadership for the church even as he supplies great natural wisdom from his experience as a practicing attorney. His primary contacts are through Rev. Rubio in Mexico and Rev. Tito Rodriguez in Honduras. Recent political calming in the country have allowed our son, Allen, and Louise to visit and teach ministerial seminars in the country and to direct medical clinics there.

PERU — 1992

"Hey. It's my dad you're looking for, not me." Allen had been invited to interpret for ministers going to Iquitos, Peru. At the time, he was pastoring near Atlanta and transferred the work to me. Of course, I knew Ken Crocker and Joe Crews, and it looked like a new door, a new opportunity. We headed south. This South American country is a part of the Latin American ministry, but it came much later in the development of missions ministry and is definitely a part of the modern era of evangelism. Iquitos is inland jungle near the headwaters of the mighty Amazon. It was the late 1980's when no highway reached the city. With constant jungle overgrowth, extensive any attempted road systems were wiped out within a month of construction. The only way in was by boat or plane. Sweltering heat and humidity, the constant climate of the area, welcomed our arrival. Peru is best known as the land of the Incas, but it is also the land of the Yawas, the Boas, of people like Rosa Vayas, of jungle river communities. The trips to Peru focused on people.

That first trip was to assist Rev. Crocker in his established work. River highways are the main routes and small independent tribes are scattered throughout the lush rainforest. I interpreted for the training seminar where we had planned to work with 25 leaders. Our presentation Bibles ran out. The constant request for more training left no doubt that we would return. But no one could have foreseen such a developed ministry of city-wide campaigns, medical clinics, training sessions, and even a floating medical ministry.

Evangelism depends on small boats and long rivers. At the first sight of the dwelling, we cut the motor and began to slide silently through the muddy waters. A call to the tribal chief. Permission to approach was granted. The long building floating on the water seemed no more than a floating raft. It was indeed a single room with hammocks and a few clothes. The 4 wives of the chief wore straw skirts and makeshift cover-ups for their chests in the presence of strangers. This man had never heard the gospel and this did not appear to be the appropriate time. It would be another year when we would return with Bibles and speak to him of spiritual things. This small group is a common social unit in the Amazon jungle. No English nor Spanish was spoken. Contact with the outside world is limited. On our second visit, a son was present who spoke Spanish. Through him, we were able to deliver the message of salvation and to present a Bible to the chief. The son's translation to his father was, "This book will tell who is Chief of all spirits. Learn of Him and get to know Him." The cultural exchange gave us a demonstration of the skills of blowgun shooting and in return for the Bible, I received a dollar bill filled with the holes from blowgun darts. Ministry among these people is costly and time consuming. Every boat trip was $250 and few care to make the tiring trip up river to search out these tiny groups.

Areas closer to Iquitos are visited more frequently by tourists and missionaries. Such tribes as the Boas are accustomed to outsiders and are more easily evangelized. They too represent the "unreached tribes" of the world. Build churches; dig wells. Though the primary focus of the church is spiritual freedom, we cannot disregard our social responsibility to the physical need. It was from Rosa and Noe that we realized that well digging was also a ministry.

Rosa impresses one first with her beauty. She is simply a beautiful young lady by anyone's standards. Her work with co-worker Noe has resulted in ten medical clinics in the city of Iquitos. As they built government sponsored clinics throughout the city, they also dug wells. People of Georgia supported these medical efforts by contributing funds and medical supplies. The Peruvian leaders supplied labor, time and educational programs on health. Here, I was a supporter. I learned — lessons on politics, lessons on life as a Peruvian. In conversation with Rosa, I learned that even far in the jungle, there is no safety from the most dangerous animals of all — man.

The conversation was casual. "Rosa, aren't you interested in marriage?" The response came quietly, almost inaudible.

"I once thought so. My 'novio' was a preacher. We were but one month from the wedding. He was cut to death on the streets of Lima. He was left in pieces, hacked to death by a machete." It was the work of the prevailing terrorist group in Peru.

The political struggles over power took her fiancé. He was killed for no more than preaching the gospel on a street corner in the capital city. The Communist rebels probably never knew him at all. He was an example — a terroristic event — a person sacrificed to produce fear. And, in Rosa's life, it produced despair. For a year, she existed in a state of despair, a broken woman unable to comprehend the "why" of the disaster. And after a year of grief, an angelic dream brought her back to her ministry. The message of the dream was "You have grieved long enough. Focus on Jesus and on His work. I am whole. I am well. Stop grieving." This was the power of vision that brought Rosa back to her ministry of building clinics and digging wells. This is the dedication of the Peruvian that will prevail as they seek their own spiritual freedom.

The Peruvian mission work is well founded in local leadership. Rev. Elias Win has been the invaluable leader in setting up city-wide evangelical services for Rev. Franklin in the Iquitos Coliseum. A training school for 88 ministers has been set up. Rev. Randall Chester and I went to teach leadership seminars to 57 workers. The interest grew to 1,100 in the 1997 seminar. With changes in the government participation in their clinics, Rosa and Noe have divided their work and now concentrate on Day Schools for the children of the city. The city of Iquitos is changing with a new airport, new roads, and new water supplies. It is also changing spiritually with major evangelistic campaigns, educational programs and social services. And, that brings us to "Chosen Vessel".

She sits on the Amazon tributary in Iquitos — three stories tall. Enter floor one for the floating hospital. Susie and Mike Dempsey were already involved in medical missions in Haiti, Honduras, and other areas when they visited Iquitos with the medical missions team from Free Chapel Worship Center. The need hit them hard. They returned to the states to sell all their investments and make the move to ministry in Iquitos. The floating hospital was their vision. For $50,000 an old boat was purchased. Repairs and remodeling made it into a river based missions center. Floor one is a hospital area, equipped with operating room and dental area. The second floor has living quarters for members of visiting medical teams. The top floor has kitchen and dining facilities. Teams of medical missionaries and spiritual teachers work on the boat in trips that average some 20 days per month. It is a place of miracles.

Louise and I have seen people stand in pouring rain for hours just to see a doctor or a nurse. Dental work and the treatment of children go on from dawn into the night. With the assistance of the city mayor, medical campaigns have moved through the city and literally saved lives. A man came in a wheelbarrow — the modern day version of a Bible story where a man was brought to Jesus by friends on a stretcher and lowered through the roof to reach the Master and be healed. (Mark 2:4) In my opinion, the man was dead. I saw no life. And yet, the friends unloaded him on a blanket and took him to the medical team. At the end of a day of IV's, he walked out of the clinic. His destination was a pulpit and his future was in gospel ministry.

AND BEYOND ...

To complete the chain from North America to South America, Panama remains. Seeds of ministry were spread there by Costa Rican workers who began a temporary work. Their return home signaled the close of the original work but not the interest. The Costa Rican conference has a zeal to evangelize and a goal to be a source of missionaries. In recent years, Rev. Juan Salazar has again made the move from Costa Rica to Panama to reopen the work there. In this effort, we have an unbroken road from the Texas border to the northern tip of South America. They all operate under national leadership. And, they simply remind us of those regions beyond — a whole continent of countries awaiting the gospel.

9

Other Horizons

AFRICA — 1962, 1998

At the sound of the name of the country, my head pounds. The steady beat of drums!!! Whether it was my first trip in 1962 to coastal Nigeria or the more inland area of Enugu, the drums are always a part of the experience. The first time, they were disturbing to me. Now, I expect them. At age 32, I approached the trip to Nigeria with apprehension. I knew nothing of the culture nor of the country. But, as the lone active missionary of the Congregational Holiness Church, I was the obvious person to evaluate the work being supported in the Nigerian interior. Native ministry under Rev. Editt had produced 33 churches and a great deal of financial support from the United States.

How different was it? Well, for one thing, Africa, the continent, is a lot bigger than Cuba, the island. As with all first visits, we seemed to travel for miles and miles to get to anything. The flight was from Atlanta to London to Lagos and then on to Calibar by small plane. At Calibar, we set out by boat for an hour and a half up the Niger River. Then a rattletrap taxi took us 40 miles to Aback, the headquarters for the churches. Three miles from Aback by bicycle and then on foot, we arrived at Rev. Editt's home. We were indeed in the jungle.

Tribal culture was maintained by clear cut rules. No two men were allowed to sleep in the same room. The result was that my traveling companion (Barnet Blalock) and I went to separate rooms a bit nervously. The community was simply working within their cultural taboos, but I was left in the dark in a very strange land, completely alone. And, those drums always started at sundown. The constant call in the night was a call to spirits in my thinking. Restful sleep was not a part of that trip.

Mealtime was totally absent — there was none. A large pot of a white root paste known as "garri" was the common food. The women would dig it up, soak it, peel it, beat it to a pulp in a hollow stump and then cook it in a large communal pot and self-served with the three fingers of the right hand. When a person was hungry, he ate. When others were hungry, they ate. There was no schedule and no utensils were available. Placed within a hut constructed of sticks and a palm thatched roof, the pot was central to the room and was constantly ready. Barnet and I survived the nine days on bananas and boiled eggs. We were constantly given items such as these as well as a goat and a chicken as offerings. Our effort to eat the chicken ended in disaster as our native friends did not know how to kill it. My North Georgia upbringing was good enough to behead a chicken. But, the boiling of it for more than an hour still produced nothing edible. It was one tough chicken!

The area was steeped in witchcraft. Later contact in Nigeria would show this influence decreased, but the effects of history always remain. In 1962, the influence was strong. Early in our visit, I was awakened at 4:00 a.m. by a shotgun blast very near my head. I was uncertain if it was inside the room or outside. The revelation of the next day was that it was indeed a blast of warning from a local witchdoctor in protest of our visit. Prayer in Nigeria came easily. Being alone at night, constant drums, strange jungle sounds, and surprises such as the shotgun blast brought me to frequent late-night prayers. The effect on the people was fear. They were a generous kind people with a desire for spiritual freedom, but they were always aware of the power of the witchdoctor. It was a political and social power as well as a spiritual power.

In worship and church services, this group was like none I had ever seen. Of course, I had been limited to U.S. church services and Latin services. They differ but they were familiar to me. The Nigerian services were highly emotional. The one musical instrument was a hollow log beaten as a drum. The "Glory March" where the women formed a train and marched around the building was common in this area. And in all their difference, there was an overwhelming sense of need and of love of spiritual things. Women brought their children at every service and insisted on prayer for them. If I left Nigeria with an impression of its people, it was that they greatly love their children. Illness and the death of children were too common. Seldom was a fully healthy strong child encountered. It was for these that the Nigerians sought strength and blessing.

The experience in Nigeria started my worldwide travels. It was my first trip outside the Western Hemisphere. It was the first time that I stood as one of only two white men ever known to spend time in that area of Nigeria. When I became ill and asked for a doctor, I was told the only doctor was 200 miles away. I returned to the U.S. through Paris and London. It was a view from the third world to the most elite of European cities within a month. I moved from jungle drums to London train sounds, from being a minority racially to being a part of the large majority, from a people hungry to hear truth and to find a better life to a population bored with the repetition of religious truth. To be a true minister to all people, I would have to be a person of constant adjustment, constant acceptance, and free of bias. The gospel message must transcend culture, language, economics, politics and any other human institutions. If Christ came for all, I must also minister to all.

The return to Africa in 1998 was a return to a much different situation. As a minister with the Free Chapel Worship Center in Gainesville, Georgia, I assisted the ministerial team in conducting city-wide services in Enugu, a more inland area of Nigeria. With the native leadership of John Huga, major campaigns had drawn as many as 100,000 persons to hear Rev. Jentezen Franklin. This more urban area quickly reflected the growth of Africa in world awareness. The government and the community accepted the group of 16 Americans interested in religious service. Response was cordial and invitations to return were rapid. However, the problems of Nigeria continue despite the strong religious work there.

Political unrest is the current enemy. On our second trip to Enugu, poverty and need were rapidly increasing. Food and supplies were becoming limited. After the death of the president of the country, political instability began to take its toll. Our five star hotel was ours to share with only 4 or 5 other guests. Our flight into the city was scheduled to leave at 10:00 a.m. but actually got underway around 5:00 p.m. Lost luggage is the norm as the passenger is responsible for checking to be sure his bags are on the flight and for finding them on arrival. And the power of witchcraft survives. As Africans move against this bondage of the past, the spiritists move underground only to rise again at the first sign of unrest in the population. One team member was constantly followed by a female spiritist who called out spells against her. The hold of curses, superstitions and spells is still strong.

For me, health was still a constant problem. The supporting prayers of the Nigerian Christians were essential to my being able to speak at the appointed seminars. And, I took home a souvenir — the bite of a brown recluse spider. The bite was unnoticed until my leg began to swell on our return trip. By London, I had a red swollen leg that looked very dangerous. By the time I returned to the U.S., doctors were puzzled at the black and yellow foot. Two of us had been bitten. Now, every itch on my lower leg serves to remind me of Africa — the land awakening, the land yearning for freedom.

LONDON — 1981

"Hispanics are lazy." "Nigerians are haughty." "English people are snobbish." These are the things one hears; they are not true. The cultural differences of any group are translated in the light of the personal culture and produce the barriers and falsehoods that often divide us. My experience as director of the Center for International Christian Ministries taught me more about cultural differences than any mission trip. We put them all into one pot and the challenge to understand one another and to work cooperatively took all my energy. It also provided a terrific learning experience. There are differences in cultures, and they always have basis in the needs of the region.

Nigerians are an aggressive people rather than haughty. Many have to struggle to survive, and this results in a remarkable ability to focus on their goals. They expect to succeed because they intend to stick to the task until it is done. This presents contention with other cultural groups, but it also ensures success. The result of this ability to focus and dedicate themselves to tasks has resulted in a high level of evangelization for their country.

South Africans vary even as their culture has divided itself so clearly. They were good students but the "colored" always kept the distance engrained in them by the Apartheid Policy of the past. (Apartheid was the South African social system that delineated whites, coloreds, Indians and blacks into distinct groups with specific regulations for each.) The South African students kept themselves emotionally separated and often appeared defensive. Insight into this group was clear and saddening. After months of battling with a young South African who seemed at constant odds with other students, I sat and confronted him with his defensiveness and inability to accept me as a friend. He simply asked how I could expect this acceptance after "a life where every contact with white people" had signaled him that he was inferior. I had no response. Courtesy from him, I could expect and did receive, but years of discrimination do not disappear with promises of friendship. Only the experience of equality will erase the wounds of generations past.

The Brazilians among us were to get along with, seldom offering confrontation, and often the first to see humor. These South Americans take life easy and do not expect change to be rapid. And, though they are European/Portuguese by background, they are "very Latin" in life style. It is a group that both Louise and I find very comfortable and amiable.

So what about Latin cultures? They tend to love to

laugh and see sociability as an essential quality. They always ask about the family and seldom move directly into business matters. They find the person and the relationship more important than economic or business matters. Of course, we were always comfortable with this group because of our years in Cuba and Latin America and because we spoke their language with ease.

The Indian students contrasted with the open, fun loving Latin culture. Years of British influence produced a people of reserve. They are not aggressive nor vocal, but they are apt to learn. Of all our students, those from India were the most successful in our program to teach others. The plan was that each students should return to his home country to teach 100 more what he had learned. The Indian student almost always accomplished this. One student even trained 800 others in the first year after his return home.

Then, there was the kind, gentle student of the Philippines. Seldom did conflict arise around these students. They were easy to get along with and anxious to be of help to others. The Indonesian culture brings the same gentleness mixed with a marked appreciation for others.

Among the Kenyan students, we found cooperation to be the hallmark. It was the English that exemplified the term "reserved." As individuals, they are helpful and responsive to direct request. However, seldom do they enjoy opening their homes to others or to unstructured social affairs. They are not the "drop in" society of the southern United States. But then, I often wonder what oddities they would assess as they look at the social characteristics of my hometown. There are those who see the American openness and sociability as insincere and "too free" in conversation. In travels, I have more than once ducked my head when hearing a loud boisterous American voice giving orders or sharing his opinion with the world at large.

I am sure that some will disagree with my assessments of different cultures, but we all base our opinions on our personal experiences. My work in London led me to work with all these cultures in a single group. All shared a commitment to Christian evangelism. And yet, there were conflicts caused by cultural differences. They key is to realize that there are differences and what one calls "snobbery" is simply respect for privacy to another. What one might call a "servile attitude" may be an expression of gentleness and appreciation of others. That which appears to our business-driven culture as "distraction" and "wasting time" is in many cultures simply good manners. No culture is better than another; they are just different.

"Center for International Christian Ministries" — it had sounded like a good idea when Rev. Bernard Underwood called me in 1981. Though he was an official with a different church denomination, our ties were close historically and spiritually. The task was fascinating — bring young national church leaders from differing countries to London and spend six months teaching them about church leadership, theological problems, establishment of churches and church growth. It was exciting to think of so much opportunity gathered in one place. A simple assignment to teach a two-week seminar was arranged so I could look over the situation and make a decision. Louise had no problem deciding. I think she prayed all through the damp cold of London that the Lord would not send us there. But the Spirit spoke differently to me. "Twenty years ago, I told you that the world would be your pulpit." It was my reminder. I had never mentioned those seemingly impossible words from the Lord to anyone. And now, He was reminding me. I knew we would be in London for some time. Thank goodness, I married a wife who willingly put aside her own discomfort for the sake of our ministry.

When the two-week session ended, our direction was clear. I had spent almost four years pastoring North Georgia churches, first in Louise's home area of Cleveland, Georgia, and then in the nearby town of Nicholson. Pastoring was a definite challenge but quite different from my missions work. Why was I there? More important, what was I learning there? It was those years of closeness to the personal lives of our church people that prepared us for the task in London. It was with some regret that I left the care of my North Georgia flock for my international flock in England. Cultures and personalities would be different, but there was a human sameness about the problems of each and the methods of dealing with them was suprisingly similar.

We moved into a large old British building that had three floors — plenty of exercise every day. Louise cooked and cleaned and cooked some more. She has always been a fantastic cook and capably adapted to cooking for six or seven nationalities. Our taste buds even became cosmopolitan. The challenge of student training has never been so difficult. The Chinese brother did not understand the system of the South African. The Nigerian did not agree with the worship common to the Indian minister. My first curriculum adjustment was the addition of a course in Cross-Cultural Communications. It was a time of learning for all of us, and the varied cultures learned to accept one another, to discuss differences, and to appreciate that every society has its specific contributions and problems in evangelism. We very literally learned from one another daily. The commitment was that each student would return and train 100 others within his own country. It was my philosophy of missions fully realized — train the national leadership to direct their own churches.

After five years, we left the work to others and returned to Georgia to take the job of Superintendent of World Missions for the church. The London experience opened doors of opportunity around the world. Over 33 different countries sent students to us, and they have provided contacts around the world for our ministry. The concepts and courses taught formed the basis for CURSUM — a training program for South and Central America. During our third year in London, my old friend June Carter (now married to Rev. Elvio Canavasio) translated the courses into Spanish. We have often traveled to assist in the teaching of these courses that have reached into Mexico, Costa Rica, Venezuela and Argentina. And, I still travel to London at least once a year to teach two-week seminars at the school in the area of World Religions and Cults, Cross-Cultural Communications, and Spiritual Warfare. The missions ministry has become "Train the National." We are but assistants to the ministry of others. As God has called us to evangelism, He also calls those of other countries and other cultures. Our task is to share, not to control.

INDIA — 1987

November 19 — 2:00 a.m. Luftansa flight #439 descends from darkness to a runway in Bombay, India. After two days and nights of travel, we thought we had arrived. It was only a stopover. The heat of the night was oppressive. A short bus ride from the international section to the domestic terminal led us to a very long wait for tickets to the city of Hydrabad. This was India and the time orientation of our western minds met head on with the event oriented society of Bombay. Things ran by events, not by the clock. When they started, they started. When events were complete, they ended. Our watches and clocks show time moving in a circular fashion. In India, those wheels moved imperceptibly slowly.

6:50 a.m. — Indian Airlines flight #119 left for Hydrabad. We were late — very late for our flight on to Rajahmundry. But our rush to catch our plane on the Russian airline Faydoot revealed the marvel of event orientation. The plane had waited for us. We settled into the small plane sorting our thoughts through the fog of jet lag. I reached with delight for the offered coffee. Foolishly, I accepted the dash of cream that made it even more enjoyable.

What a greeting in Rajamundry! Over a hundred Christian "friends" met us with songs and music. Garlands of flowers, heavy with weight and with perfume, were tossed around our necks. A sign stretched across the airport entrance with each of our names and a major "Welcome" announcing our arrival. Rev. and Mrs. Victor who had visited us in the U.S. on several occasions were on hand to greet us. They rushed us to a hotel where other signs of welcome greeted us. It certainly was not a quiet entry into Rajamundry. It was as great an outpouring of affection and welcome as I have ever received. It was typical of the entire time with our Christian friends in India. These are a gracious and thoughtful people. Flower garlands, refreshment, and personal kindness were constant.

City life in India is full. There is no extra space, no quiet little stopping spot. Activity is constant. I'm sure that someone looking down from a great height would see those streets as filled with the busiest colony of ants one can imagine. We were in a typical Indian city. A world of gurus, religious mystics, temples with idols, fortune tellers, snake charmers, and the overriding sounds of worship calls. Streets were crowded with animals, trash, squalor and multitudes of people. Strange smells mixed with the not-so-strange. Voices of calling vendors and beggars mixed with sounds of spitting, of clearing throats, and the blowing out of nostrils. Wealth and poverty stood elbow to elbow. The living stepped over the dying. Mud huts leaned precariously toward opulent palaces.

Jet lag still had its hold on us, but we managed a trip downtown to see the sights. Passing under the multi-armed god who guarded the area, I found the fullness of Indian urban life before me. To say the street was "full" is a terrible understatement. People, cows, bulls, dogs, hogs and rickshaws moved with the flow of bicycles and ox carts. Beggars cried for help while children stared at the foreigners. Food vendors sold coconuts, fruits, spices, bananas and a myriad of things past my knowledge. Most necessities were available from the small stores that lined both sides of the narrow roadway. It was like a boiling stew with every ingredient ever experienced bubbling in the mix.

From this street, the dichotomy of Indian religion was clear as the Hindu idol stretched his many arms over the entry to the street, and the Muslim mosque pointed its spires upward at the other end. These are the two religions of India and they are as opposite as can be found among the beliefs of man. Though Ghandi tried to reconcile the two, he failed. The fundamental differences and their natural forms of expression can only bring conflict of belief and of followers.

The Moslem faith is based on a belief in one god whose name is Allah. His prophet was Mohammed, and the principles of the religion are clearly written in the precise text of the Koran. By contrast, Hinduism is a religion without a founder. It is a revealed truth, a dogma, a structured liturgy. For the Muslim, God is a Creator standing apart from his creation, ordering and presiding over his work. To the Hindu, the creator and his creation are one and indivisible, embodied in an all pervading cosmic spirit whose manifestations are unlimited. The Muslim worships in a mosque where any representation of god in painting or sculpture is forbidden. The idol is blasphemous among the Muslim. And, the Hindu temple is filled with representations and idols of gods in all their possible forms. They worship animals, ancestors, spirits, natural forces, and divine incarnations as embodiments of their gods. To the Hindu, a god may be manifested in the snake, in water, in fire, in stars and planets, in the thunder of the night or the cow that walks down the street. This is India. The contrast is almost incomprehensible, and yet the people live in the midst of it choosing what they will believe and rejecting what defiles their belief. It is no wonder that Christian ministry is a long process. Another god, another religion — they make very little impact on the Indian mind. The Muslim rejects totally anything outside the Koran. The Hindu finds no quarrel with a new God or new religion but sees it as an addition to and not a replacement for the old gods.

Mission work is done by persons willing to leave the comforts of a known homeland to live in strange circumstances. But lasting works are the result of local people of long-term commitment and dedication. Rev. and Mrs. Victor gave a lifetime to ministry in their native India. And, in one of the hardest countries to evangelize, they have built a collection of churches and strong centers of Christian faith. Some churches were well constructed buildings, but more often we met in small buildings made of mud and thatched roofs. Open sewers ran nearby. Others services were in the open air because crowds were too large for the churches. Those attending were always attentive, kind, and responsive. Requests for prayer were constant. In indescribable poverty, these people took time to worship.

One evening service had so many attending that we met outside the church. I well remember the gifts of refreshing drinks, bananas and more garlands of flowers. I also recall the "uninvited guests" which included rats, bugs, roaches, and other crawling things. Few of them seem to have been moved by my preaching. Another memorable service was among a group of converted Hindus in a lantern-lit church. Monsoon rains found us driving through three feet of water to reach the village. We were greeted with such fervor that the trip back along dark roads filled with unlit ox-carts, bicycles and other vehicles hardly shook us at all.

For most of the sixteen days there, I was plagued by jet lag and weakness. The coffee cream on my plane trip proved to be less than healthy, and the result was fairly constant diarrhea, stomach pains, and my recurring tendency to nose bleeds. Yet among all the peoples I have visited, none are more thoughtful and welcoming than those of India. Rev. Joe Crews, Rev. Kenneth Law and I would awaken at 4:30 or 5:00 a.m., heat up our little stove and start the water for coffee. By early morning, we would have our bodies nearly awake and operational for travel and ministry. Rev. Terry Crews was his usual hearty self after a few days of trying to sleep off the 24 hours of plane travel to get to Rajamundry. Jet lag feels similar to the effect of having 20 lbs. of extra weight attached to your body and living in slow motion.

Two of our most notable days included a service of uplifting service of praise, preaching and prayer with over a hundred Indian Christians. The church was in one of the best built of the structures we had visited. It was, however, the baptistry in one corner that was impressive. Water baptism is a solemn decision for converts in most countries and especially in India. It usually only occurs some time after conversion as it is truly a sacred step of public commitment. More than once, the service of water baptism alone has resulted in total expulsion from one's family. On a second day of note, it was our travel to and from service that provided the outstanding memories. Mud claimed our car before we reached the village so we walked the remaining portion. An excited congregation and a gracious pastor made it worth the effort. Then, with the help of a local farmer, we were able to free our car from the mud and head back to town. A lunch stop at a local restaurant became an opportunity to pray for a man suffering with a large ugly sore on his leg. Having eaten our meal on plates that were actually banana leaves, we were not too pleased to realize that the cook and owner was indeed the man with the running sore. It was an area where there were few tourists, and we were learning "when in India do as the Indians do."

Our purpose in India was to officially organize The Congregational Holiness Church of India. Of course, the churches had existed and had been effective for several years. However, a conference with appropriate local leadership and governance was now set in order. Sixteen pastors gathered with us at the central church in Rajahmundry for an open question/answer session before the service. Clarification of church discipline and organizational methods were clarified to everyone's satisfaction. The service was held in a large tent adjacent to the church. I preached as Rev. Victor interpreted and at the close of the sermon, the conference was set in order. It was a day of VICTORY; our purpose for this trip was complete. A meal of rice and curry for over 400 people was served after the service. We later shared a fine restaurant meal in celebration of Rev. Victor's birthday. His wife had saved for this special gift to him, and we were happy to share it.

Every place visited is special. Every place is different. India is almost an opposite of our Latin American works in the culture of the people, the customs, the procedures. And yet, there is a sameness in the people. There is the kindness of Christian love, a willingness to reach out, and a dedicated group of church leaders giving their everyday lives to minister to those around them. I long remember the countries, the sights, the noises, the smells. But, the faces of the people and the spirit of love that return to me go past memory and into my heart. After all theses years, I can still close my eyes and feel the warmth.

UKRAINE — 1999

Denge Fever! Again! No, it is not possible. Denge Fever is not recurring. Once you've had it, it's done. Well, actually I seem to be part of a new trend. People can have recurrence of Denge, and I'm one of those proving it. So, in the midst of one of our planet's most civilized countries, I lie on a sofa in London, England, weakened with the fever. Allen and I came for a week of teaching. It was a week of rising from bed to teach and returning as soon as it was over. And, then we're off to the Ukraine.

Since the fall of the Soviet Union, the scattered countries of the area all have independent governments. The Ukraine openly invites evangelism and ministry giving our friend Slavic Radchuk great influence among church and political leaders. We were now making our third trip to teach and train ministers. Neither Allen nor I spoke the language, but that was not a concern. We had good interpreters and had confirmed our arrival time by e-mail.

The airport was like that of dozens of struggling countries ... directions for foreigners were unclear, people from many countries were speaking varied languages and searching the unfamiliar signs for a recognizable word or phrase. Finding anyone who could speak the remotest form of English was a challenge. A country trying to redirect itself and fight off the mafia control had more important things to do than provide "tourist services" for incoming guests. Scanning the crowds for the third and fourth time, we found no familiar face. Where was our contact? Several hours later, it was clear that no one would be coming for us. We had to come to some decision. Staying in the airport was not an option. "Son, we have to do something. I can't sit up much longer. Shall we get a hotel for the night or a taxi out to Rivne to look for the school."

Though the taxi ride was 5 1/2 hours, it was as cheap as a hotel room so we elected to head for the city of Rivne where we could surely get information on the location of the school. That was about my fourth or fifth miscalculation of the evening. Arrival in Rivne found us driving up and down streets with no addresses and no one who could understand enough English to help us.

"Seminary?"   "Seminario Mision?"   "Seminao Misoe?" I was trying all three of the languages I knew and getting no where. I had stopped our wandering taxi at the largest hotel I could find with the assumption that surely someone here would speak a little English. Wrong! No English. After gestures, pantomime and a childish drawing of a church with a cross, we arrived at the idea of church.

"Catholic?"

" No! Protestant!"

Aha! A glimmer of recognition. Now the words for school or seminary. English, Spanish, Portuguese — and just a hint of a flicker in the eye indicated we might be making progress.

Seminario Mision?

"Yes!!"

My nodding head got the message across. Out came the phone book and the call was made. From the information operator, our friendly desk clerk progressed to another call. Then the pantomime of fingers — one, two, five — five fingers. Did she mean five minutes or five hours? All we were sure of was that we were to wait. I settled back into a peace born not of confidence but of the knowledge that I could do no more. Our contact appeared shortly, and we were on the final leg of our journey. It was nowhere near the first time I had leaned my head back against a car seat and wished for Louise and home. God's calling is precious, and I would have my life no other way than this. But, my longing for the peace of home and the comfort of my bed and my wife's cooking almost overwhelmed me in the stress of the work.

The week in the Ukraine was marvelously productive. We taught daily and went to very structured services in the evenings. All visiting ministers are invited to give full-length sermons. The result was often a service of three to four hours with strict attention to sermons in a language we did not understand. With the new freedom to worship, people came in droves. From the smaller churches of 250 to the large auditorium services of over 3,500, every service was packed to the limit. The response of the people made hard-backed chairs and rigid posture into joyous circumstances. With my fever still raging, I staggered from place to place physically exhausted. However, my inner self was almost leaping with joy.

The fears of revolutionary days in Cuba returned every time we were stopped by a mafia group on the highway. Guns scare me, especially when they point at me. However, the automobile stops were common and the night view of a sight of a lighted road barricade meant another session with mafia thugs. We had no real problems but every time it happened, our Ukraine speaking driver would be taken away for questions and we would be left in the car to wonder if they would come back for us, would our driver return, what could we possibly do. But, each time, the driver did return and we would continue to our destination — or to another mafia stop.

None of these things erase the wonder of the people and the church work. We had spent our previous trips to the area with large ministerial campaigns. The crowds were tremendous and the most impressive work had been among prisons. In one women's prison, we were allowed services with over 1200 women. A year later, we returned to find active Bible studies and religious television common in the prison. In the men's prison, things were not as quickly accepted. The beginning was hostile and ridicule from a "tough bunch" was our reception. However, even that atmosphere broke into acceptance with continued ministry.

This trip was a teaching trip. The need for training of ministers in the Ukraine is the mission. With our plan to have four seminars yearly and to train a selected group of 25 pastors each year, great progress is being made. The Ukrainian people have a deep commitment to the Lord but worship is influenced by a tradition of non-emotional legalistic religion based in the Greek Orthodox Church. Services are lengthy and formal. The minimum four or five sermons are given at each service where the congregation sits erect and motionless. Women and men sit separately, no one leaves early for any cause, and the only emotion expressed is through weeping. Women sit with heads covered; men sit at attention. There is no music. But the strains of the a capella choirs and the fervency of prayer move the soul. These are people who have suffered beyond our concept. Their spiritual lives have been guarded and controlled. From the years of Communist pressure, a strong pure wine of spiritual fullness has come forth. These people know the suffering of the Gospel and the power of their prayers is a power born of that suffering.

The current atmosphere is an open acceptance of the Gospel. Television was mandated for every family during the Communist regime presenting an effective means of communication. American ministry is known throughout the area. Slavic's weekly religious program is the highest rating program in the Ukraine. Our training program involves 25 pastors each year and three sessions of training, followed by salary support and a church building program. In the first year, over 50 pastors have been trained and 35 churches were built. Every service is packed to capacity. In auditoriums seating 3,500, we ministered to standing room only crowds. With fever or without, I taught five hours daily and attended lengthy evening services somewhere every night.

Life in the Ukraine is hard. Our orphanage work tries to shelter street children, snatched from the underground tunnels where they sleep on top of the steam lines to keep warm. Wages are $1 per day for most workers. Medical doctors receive $70 a month — when they get paid. It is never certain that paychecks will come or that goods will be available for purchase. The Ukraine is the "breadbasket of Europe" with beautiful fields and food growing in every yard. Yet, life is a struggle for food and clothing. Winters are harsh and loss of government control means freedom for all, but a freedom for lawlessness as well. The mafia controls through force. Farmers headed to market frequently lose crops or portions of them to the tariffs of clear "highway robbery". No one moves through the countryside for any cause without traversing a minefield of thugs and "authorities" created by ownership of a gun. Communism was the evil that kept these people under control for decades, but the movement to freedom and self-determination is not a smooth road. It is a road for courageous people. The Ukrainians will survive, and they will prevail. They have learned the power of patience and an inner faith that will not be broken.

L to R: (p. 140) Hugh & Louise dedicate church in Reynosa, Mexico, teaching in Guatemala, witnessing in Peru (p. 141) Desk work, with Elias Magana in Mexico, Missionary Training Center summer group.

Part III
The People

*Pillars of Strength
Those Gone By...*

10

Pillars of Strength

The ministry is always about people. It is never just projects or buildings. The beauty of Cuba, the excitement of different cultures, and the wonder of other ways of life interest me greatly. But, the call is to the people for they are all interesting, each so very unique, every one a connection to the spirit within me. But, as my outreach has been to people, those who stood with me and supported me are almost like the promise to Abraham of blessings as "stars in the heavens" or "sand upon the sea shore" (Gen. 22:17). To name the individuals who have walked with me and sustained me in my work would be impossible. However, in my weakness, there have been three special ones who stood in the gap and filled me with strength on a daily basis.

LOUISE: The Beloved

"Hermana. ¿Cómo estás?" It was a pretty standard greeting for **Louise Skelton**. This wife of mine was always the first out to meet and to talk with people. In our years of church planting, Louise started with the women and children and developed Sunday Schools and backyard Bible Schools. It was from those that we advanced to church services and family worship. She began ministering in Cuba before I did and learned Spanish well before me. Still today, she is the first to step in to coordinate travel needs, to translate and even to preach for me when illness prevents my continuing.

As a helpmate, she has always been willing to pack up and move even when she didn't really like our destinations. She stopped counting the moves after the first 35. With less than two years in that first little cottage in Florida, she packed up for travel to the unknown of the Texas border and Mexican ministry. Though she learned to love London and its people, she literally endured our years there in the cold that chilled her to the bone. Despite her talents in ministry, she has been faithful to the ministry of cooking, cleaning, and hosting an actual multitude of visitors over the years. And, as one of our friends puts it, "Louise can make Campbell's soup taste like a gourmet meal."

Born the 9th of 12 children in White County, Georgia, Louise learned Christian devotion from her parents. They always went to the Union Grove church. She remembers well that they lived in White County on White Creek where no blacks were allowed. But, life on their farm was different. Her father hired black farm workers every season who were always invited to share at the family table. Prejudice was not tolerated in their home.

As a minister's wife, she has never rejected whatever role came her way. She is faithful to minister to whatever need presents itself whether it is praying for the sick, teaching Sunday School, counseling, or cooking. But, she has her own ministry too. Her call to minister that sent her to Cuba has continued to lead her to Christian leadership. She is active in women's ministries as guide and translator on trips to Central America, Mexico and Cuba. While we work in the conferences with pastors, Louise is usually busy with organizing women's ministries to complement them. On medical missions trips along the Amazon, she has her special ministry of spiritual encouragement and evangelism. Of all the influences of my ministry, none has been so strong and so constant as that of my wife. Perhaps I should let her tell her story this way.

I (Louise) remember Hugh from our teen years, but we had no real relationship then. It was his sister who was my friend. But, Dorothy married and moved to Cuba while I went to work at an office in Gainesville, Georgia. I felt the need for more education and enrolled at a University of Georgia off-campus center at night. Little did I know that it would take three colleges and many years before I could finish that B. A. degree in Spanish at Pan American University in south Texas. During that time, I developed tuberculosis, a common and serious illness of that particular era. First, I stayed with my sister and then was sent to Battey State Hospital in Rome, Georgia. This tubercular sanitarium was home for four long months. It was not at all pleasant but did give me a lot of time for prayer and Bible study. A letter from Dorothy (Hugh's sister) put a seed of desire in my mind. Dorothy wrote, "Come over here and stay with us. The climate is good. I'll take care of you until you get your strength back." It was more than a new idea; it was the beginning of God's call to lifelong ministry in missions.

What was I to do? What was the wise thing to do? What was the spiritually correct thing to do? All these questions filled my days. As I sat down at the Thanksgiving meal, my appetite left me. I would know no peace until I made steps to go to Cuba. Air treatments were common for conditions such as mine, but I steadfastly refused them. This was not what God had planned for me.

The heavy feeling of Thanksgiving Day stayed with me until the day I left the hospital. Doctors were perplexed at my refusal of certain treatments and finally called my sister to come for me.

I returned to my parents' home in White County and stayed until April when Hugh Skelton (my friend's brother) came to take me to the airport in Atlanta. Before that day, my sister asked me to go back to the specialist who had diagnosed my illness for a check up. The same physician who had diagnosed the tuberculosis was astonished. He marveled at the progress of my health, of how fortunate I was, and prescribed resuming my activities with a minimum of two hours rest per day. Even my concerned sister could find no reason to keep me from my appointed flight to Cuba.

I stayed in Cuba with Dorothy and her family for 14 months. I was learning the work of a missionary, learning a language I had never spoken before. How well I remember my proud purchase of a Berlitz Spanish book before I left and how pleased I was going to be when I stepped off that plane communicating with the Cuban people so well. Of course, I had only read the book and never heard the language. My pronunciation was no where near a Spanish sound, and there was little doubt that I would need some language lessons as soon as possible. Following some good advice, I began attending an elementary school. I sat in a 4th grade classroom every morning for four months at a private Baptist school. The afternoons were spent putting my language learning into practice on visits to local families. From this, I started teaching the small children in church. I assumed my life's work had begun. I would be a missionary in Cuba – forever.

After eight months on the island, we had the excitement of a visit from Hugh and another minister. It was good to see old friends and have news from home. During his visit, Hugh realized his own spiritual call to missionary ministry. We began to fall in love. "Goodness," my thoughts told me, "If I marry Hugh, I won't even get to change my last name." It was not long after he returned to the states that I received a letter proposing marriage. Though he was certainly attractive, marriage was more serious to me than teasing and dreaming. We had not dated a great deal – mostly double dates and friendship dates. I could remember his walking me home from college classes so I could advise him with his girlfriend problems.

But, I had begun to love him. Our paths were destined by God, and they led in the same direction. This was as surely my spiritual destiny as missionary work in Cuba. Hugh insists that I took a long time to answer that letter, but I answered in exactly the right timing and the answer was, "Yes." I returned to Georgia to marry him and to spend our next few years in college, in pastoral work, and in having a son. But, all that time was focused toward our goal of returning to Cuba.

Cuba was the beginning. Life with Hugh was a constant move after that. I chose to look forward to the exciting new ministries rather than long for the past. Those places and events are written about earlier in this book. I can only add some personal impressions, some lessons in life, that I learned along the way.

From Cuba, I learned cultures and ethnic differences. It was my first experience in a foreign country. The racial mixture that worked so cooperatively impressed me. We were totally accepted, and even with the years of revolution and constant shelling in our area, I knew few times of fear. It was such a time of learning for me – a new language, a new culture, a different way of life. The Cubans worked around their many superstitions. If they ironed in the daytime, they would not go out in the moonlight. It was odd, but not so different from folks who avoid walking under ladders or school children who try not to "step on a crack and break your mother's back". I best remember Cuba as a place where we were happy. The people were loving and pleasant. On my return for a visit in 1998, I found them still a happy group. The current poverty and hardships still have not undermined their positive attitude or sense of humor.

In Texas and Mexico, I learned adjustment. Even the vocabulary of the Spanish spoken there required adjustment. People in this area were slower to accept Americans. It was there that I learned to entertain guests in large groups and to handle much more complex social situations. As we lived in Texas and worked with churches in Mexico, we were in constant cultural adjustment. Of course, those were major child rearing years. When you have only one child, you get no practice time in guiding their lives. It was a time of family stress as we attempted to devote our time to missions and deal with a typical PK (Preacher's Kid) trying to shed the image forced upon him.

London was my inner struggle time. I did not want to go to that cold wet climate. I really did not want to be "matron" to large multi-cultural student group plus the Center staff. I did not want to cook for 30 people every meal. But, despite my prayers, we did go there. The school had a mixed enrollment from such places as China, South Africa, England, India, the Philippines, etc. in its average term. What did I learn? I learned that American meals don't please everyone. It was a struggle for six week as I secretly longed for a "breakdown" so I could go home gracefully. But, I was where God meant for me to me, and in reading the last chapter of John I found Jesus cooking fish on the seashore. Jesus cooked too. And he said to John, "Do you love me? Feed my sheep." It was a turning point for me — an attitude change.

The change was that I began to stop being "the Director's Wife" and the kitchen martyr and became a friend. I began to see the opportunities for learning as well as for ministry. Including the students in the cooking process gave them pleasure. I was relieved of some work and enjoyed learning to cook from a global cookbook. I learned that rice is the universal food, and you must cook it for every meal. The students cooked once a week with their choice of cuisine. And, they began to help out on other days also. When the second year came, we were able to hire some help with the house chores, and I had come to enjoy the colorful daily life of an international school.

Another thing I learned well in London was the ugliness of racial prejudice. Though born and raised in the South, my parents had never expressed or tolerated prejudice. It existed in other places we lived, but we were basically protected from it. We moved from group to group with little awareness of tensions between them. But, the South Africans who came to our school in London were very aware of racial bias. In the park, I took a seat beside a black student without thought. He was the one who had to adjust. His comment later was that it was not easy for him because in his country, "I could never sit by a white woman." We saw conflict between our students based on old customs of prejudice that had to be dealt with. It was in this place that I learned to listen and watch for prejudice and to move to counteract it at every chance.

London began as a struggle for me. It ended with the knowledge that if we had not gone there, I would have missed some of the greatest days of my life. The missionary call is to "Go into all the world." We were able to minister in London and see the world come to us for teaching and training. We learned as we taught. My greatest lesson there was of tolerance. No matter what the cultures, we can live together in harmony. God loves us all, and we can learn to be as one family within Him.

After London, I had learned to be content wherever we were. I saw more clearly that what I would prefer was not what was best for me. In the following years of administrative work, I learned that time was precious and there would be very little of it for our personal pleasures. With our move to a base in Georgia, we began to develop strong local friendships and more permanent personal ties. I now get to teach Spanish in small groups as well as through the church. It seems that we are now working in the areas for which we were prepared. Life is not dull or less busy. In fact, we seem busier than ever. But, we are "properly fitted" into the ministry that now fills our lives.

JOSE: The Son Become Father

The greatest of "con" men, a thug, and an alcoholic – he was always good at what he chose to do. Few people would recognize this respected minister and family man as what he was then. Cantabria, Mexico is not on the tourist route. It is a tiny village in the mountain area of Michoacan. And the poorest of the poor was the household into which he was born. The large Rubio family was raised among farmers with a strong Christian influence that had little impact on the teen-aged Jose. Running with the gangs and thugs of the area, he wanted out of the poverty. And he found that the best way to get ahead was to take what he wanted – or to get someone to give it to him. Jose deceptively convinced the mayor of the nearby city of Morelia that he was a poor orphan in need of education and lied his way into an exceptional government school. Thus, his education and training were superb. His communist alma mater taught only the best.

But even quality education could not hold his interest for long. Jose left school early and drank long. It was not long before he made his move to the northern town of Reynosa looking for that "border action". As he looked for "action", he found Christ — and I found a friend for life. An invitation to a Protestant service ended with conversion and a commitment to Christian service. His polished intelligence immediately steered him toward Bible School. His persuasive practice was quickly put into use. When the Bible School director refused his entry for a year so that Jose could "prove himself" as a Christian, it was not acceptable.

"Brother Stone. If I die today, will I go to heaven?"

"Of course, Jose, " replied the director.

"Then if I am qualified to go to heaven, why am I not qualified to go to your Bible School?"

Jose was immediately enrolled and became a most excellent student as well as successful graduate. As he traveled the road to education, I had begun my journey toward establishing an evangelical work in Mexico. Our roads met. Mexican regulations forbid foreign-led religious activities. So, I needed a national worker to establish things, and Jose was recommended. Neither of us realized how close and long this friendship would become. We began with Jose and Louise going into the barrios of Reynosa, inviting children and eventually the mothers to Sunday School. From that stretched canvas cover in the Beltran's backyard grew a church and eventually an entire network of churches plus a Bible School in the country of Mexico. The unruly border ruffian named Jose became the superintendent of that sister conference in Mexico which now includes 230 churches or more.

Rubio began working in the ministry with 1 shirt and 1 pair of pants. And, even then, his "flaw" was his generosity. If he traveled to Georgia with me and was given clothes, they were given away almost as soon as he got to Mexico. He literally gave his shoes away one day because "I have two pair and he had none." In the early days of Mexican ministry, we went to a jail for service. After Jose preached, one shirtless prisoner challenged him. "It's easy for you to preach this gospel, you have clothes to wear and a good life." Jose simply removed his shirt and gave it to the man.

In addition to generosity, Jose is a man of pride. Seldom would he ask for anything and then never for himself. I once sat in service where he was to preach and noted his tearfulness. He quietly told me I would have to minister in his place. "Why, Jose? What's the matter?" He was sick from not eating for three days. He would ask neither me nor his church congregation for food. From Jose, I learned the ways of Latin America. I learned to be patient, to listen, to have faith in the goodness and the wisdom of the native leadership. His own keen leadership skills and personal contacts led us to strong church work and a Bible School in Morelia, Mexico. Though he was not experienced in religious work, Jose was quick to learn and wise to know when he needed to ask questions of others. And, he believed in what he was doing. From that alcoholic thug, Jose became a helper, a pastor and now the leader of a national ministry. As a radio evangelist, he is known throughout Mexico, and his generous nature founded one of the greatest Bible distribution ministries known to Mexico and Central America. Today, Jose Rubio serves as Field Representative of Latin America which includes church conferences in Guatemala, Honduras, Costa Rica, El Salvador and Nicaragua, Panama, Venezuela, and Chile. As we began ministry in Brazil, Jose was with me to assist. He was our first re-contact with Cuba, making several trips to visit the Christian families there.

Jose married well. When he married Mary Serna, he completed a dream and began a beautiful family. She works beside him or without him when he is away, as is frequently the case. If anyone were to be envious of Jose, it would be for the wife and three lovely daughters who so deeply love and respect him. From the streets of Cantabria, he has risen to a place of respect among the masses, to leadership among leaders, and to being beloved by those he loves most. Without him, the major portion of my work in Latin America would have been impossible. We have been together in danger, in tribulation, and in victory. He has walked with me through large cities and major meetings as well as through jungle trails and mountain heights. And, as a true son to me, he has done nothing greater than lead my own son into spiritual ministry beyond my comprehension.

It was Jose who first took my son to Central America as a minister. As the "elder brother," he taught Allen to laugh, to cry, to pray, to preach. He led him through experiences that taught him that ministry is less preaching and more praying, less leading than serving. Through this friend's compassion and total unselfishness, we all learned to see the people of the mission field and not the projects. As a confidante, a guide, and an admonisher in the Word, he is unsurpassed.

ALLEN: The Future

Well, a son is a good thing to have. Our young marriage was thrilled with the birth of Hugh Allen Skelton while we were in Macon, Georgia. Being young in marriage, in the ministry, and just generally "young", we thought nothing of taking the baby to Cuba at the age of 11 months. Though our field of missions changed several times, Allen was always with us until the age of 18. He thought his return to Georgia at that age meant he had had left missionary work forever. However, at age 42, he has returned to full-time work as an evangelist and teacher in missions schools throughout the world. This outgoing prankster named Allen was not exactly the image of his father in those early days. Much of his early life was spent in the streets of Latin countries and at the corner "bodega" while we were having church services. Bi-culturalism was natural to him, and the conflict of normal teen-age struggles and religiously principled parents was not made easy with a father that was gone more than home. Allen says he hardly ever remembers his father throwing a ball with him or taking him fishing. As parents, Louise and I remember only our concerns for this beloved son who needed both freedom to become his own person but also protection from life in a town where things "illegal" became available and acceptable with a 20 minute drive across the border to Mexico. With the mixed emotion that most parents experience, we supported his leaving south Texas for north Georgia and the decisions of adulthood.

The years that followed were less stormy but still unsteady. He moved from training as a meat cutter to computer training and then to a job with a national company maintaining their computer systems. The job gave him plenty of time between "emergencies" and led to a real examination of himself and his goals. Allen's personal commitment to the Lord at age 20 had brought a real peace to our lives, and we were quite content to see him as an active member of his local church. Of course, we were parents enough to constantly be looking for that "right girl" in his life. It was during these years that his mother casually asked, "Why don't you go down and take Vicky Jimmerson out?"

Allen had met Vicky at our Training Center in Texas some years back, and the attraction to her had been evident. He made the trip to Griffin, Georgia, and many more followed. Their marriage and their three children have led me into a whole new world of grandfathering. Each of our grandchildren is so different and yet so special. Starla was the firstborn dependable darling that has become a beautiful young lady. Bethany is the quick creative child that responds to every minute of life. And, Buddy is the young athlete filling every moment with activity.

In those early years of family life, Allen had begun extensive study during his "down time" on the job and had moved into church service as an assistant pastor at his home church. When the pastor left for other ministry, Allen became the senior minister in a downtown Atlanta church. In his years there, the church moved to the suburbs and grew into a stable strong church and a full-time job for Allen and Vicky. Those years were filled with growth as a counselor, teacher, minister and administrator. And yet, those looking at his life from the outside began to see the clarity of a call to missions. Louise and I dared not even think of what it might be. It was enough to pray, "Lord, Thy will be done!" No error is worse than directing persons into ministries to which they have no true spiritual leading. When it was the right time for them, Allen announced his decision to leave the church for full-time work in missions and founded White Field's Ministry. It was a move that almost everyone saw before he did. During his pastoral years, Allen was active in taking youth groups to minister in Mexico and in teaching at Latin American Conferences. He had become a leader in the missions effort. The step to leaving his church and steady salary for a work dependent on gifts and contributions was not an easy one. He and Vicky had three children to support, and the oldest was nearing college age. Nevertheless, it was the time, and there is no choice but to follow when a family has committed themselves to the Lord's guidance.

The success of Allen's ministry is another book altogether. But, his assistance to me personally and professionally has been beyond words. We talk often of our various ministries. There is no greater pleasure than ministering with him. The sameness of our backgrounds and theology make us good "growing partners". His great differences from me make our journeys enjoyable and exciting. I am a constant; he is unpredictable. I sit and laugh inwardly; he is the center of humor in any gathering. We carry the same burden of ministry and make a good "team". But, he far outshines my personality and ability to entertain. A son is a good thing to have, and I am of all men most blessed.

11

Those Gone By . . .

People pray for you when you don't know it. Others send checks when they don't know why. Friends keep watch over your family or your property while you are away. In the field, people give you their last eggs for a meal or gather their pennies to be sure coffee is present when you arrive at their homes. Native ministers spend nights in prayer or travel through mud trails in beaten up trucks to prepare for the service you will attend. It is impossible to mention the many contributions and the many people who have made my work possible. So, when I look back and feel at all successful in fulfilling my call to the ministry, I realize that I am so blessed to have friends that made it happen.

There are the many many friends who support Louise and me constantly — enough to fill more volumes than we can print. But, most of those friends are still writing their stories. They continue faithful in service. Their stories are not finished yet so they are not written here. However, there are also those whose work in this realm of life is finished, and I would remind you of them.

Elmer Moreira

The end came on a rain-slick road in rural Alabama. It was far from the lush island beauty of his native Cuba. In my first ministry, the young Cuban had been my guide, my teacher, and my friend. Elmer supplied the link that only a native pastor can bring to the ministry. We rode over dusty roads and walked through military terrors, but I was not there when the panel truck overturned, and he was lost to us forever.

I remember him as a young and learned man, always positive, always smiling. This handsome Latin with light, already thinning, hair had an appearance of strength and leadership. His work bore out those attributes. Elmer was not an easily frightened person but I well remember a day when we were both shaken so badly that we could barely drive home. We had entered the bar to discuss renting a house for the Moreiras, and all seemed normal — except for the straight-backed men who watched every movement. They wore no uniforms but were definitely men of violence, Batista's men. Having completed our negotiations, I headed for the car not hearing the command to "come back here". Elmer heard and obeyed immediately. Near the middle of the road outside, I turned to see the gun pointed at my head.

"Didn't you hear me?"

"No. Did I do something wrong?"

Within three minutes, the secret police arrived, six soldiers with guns and sirens. The accusation was criticism against the government of Batista, and their procedure was to circle us menacingly. I prayed and took a chance. That one, he was the leader. I would speak to him.

"Este Señor es un pastor. We are only seeking to rent a house for my friend. We have nothing to do with the revolution." I produced papers to prove my missionary status and continued to plead my case gently. It worked! I was released.

"You may go." However, Elmer was to stay.

I stood at the car for the longest time — waiting, praying, wondering. And, as I waited, Elmer received the tongue lashing of a lifetime. The soldiers berated him for everything from his heritage to his imagined political ideals before they released him. They intended to frighten him, and they succeeded. As he approached the car, he was visibly shaken. It was not a safe country for anyone. We left in silence, once again aware of the uncertainty of life and how powerless we were as humans in an inhuman situation.

Elmer and his wife, Sara, ministered in Santiago. They evangelized, pastored, and provided leadership for the expanding church organization. It was while traveling through the southern United States on a fund-raising trip for us that Elmer was trapped. He was trapped on the northern side of the tiny passage between Miami and Cuba, and his family was on the southern side. The revolution closed the doors to his return and left him with many anxious months before the rest of his family was brought out to join him.

Reunited, the Moreiras began to seek their place in the ministry once again. Though Elmer was steadily working at missions efforts as a translator with the T. L. Osborne Association, he felt the need to work more directly with people. In 1967, he resigned the Tulsa job and began his move to become a missionary to the Central American country of Honduras.

"I used to drive one of these vans in Cuba. Let me drive it a while." Elmer was always anxious to help out so he drove as the rains began. Then came an area of road construction. New paving had left the unfinished road edges with sharp edges. A wheel slipped off the raised lane, and the vehicle spun out of control. There was no doubt that death came instantly. The gentle, educated man from Cuba would not preach his masterful sermons to the people of Honduras. The work of future ministry would be left to his eldest son, far far down the road of life beyond our ability to see.

Nona Jo Alvarado

Ray and Nona Jo did not find their way to the mission field as youngsters. They were in their 40's when they decided to serve the church missions effort. Ray spoke Spanish from childhood, but Nona Jo had to struggle with it. Their missionary effort was marked by a willingness to serve where needed. At that time, it was Honduras.

Honduras is a small Central American country. It is not wealthy nor industrially developed. It is, in fact, a country of gentle people seeking to snatch their livelihood from the steamy jungles or the rugged mountains. The influence of hurricanes is more than the influence of tourists. And, it was to San Pedro Sula that Ray and Jo went to develop a church work.

During their years of work, they helped establish a lasting church work. More importantly, they assisted in developing a core of native workers of such strength that the ministry of exciting evangelism and Bible education continued under native leadership after they left. If you want to feel the energy of an excited church people, visit Honduras. If you want to find faith as you have seldom seen it, travel among the evangelical churches of Honduras. This was the work to which Nona Jo and Ray gave their years of work.

When they left Honduras to return to the area of Atlanta, Georgia, they brought their adopted son, "Paco" with them. Nona Jo was not well. Her diabetes was out of control, and the years ahead would be physically difficult. In her decline, the thing that was constant was her love of the church and of her family. She carried the work in her heart when her body could not respond to the call. Her legacy lives on in "Paco" as he works with the children's ministry and the outreach ministry of his local church.

L. M. Reese

This young man from small town south Georgia could study his language dictionary longer than I could study my Bible. And, that is not to say that he neglected his Biblical studies. Leon Reese (L. M.) was a man of discipline. With his bride, Beverly, he was ready to tackle one of our most difficult missions areas. In 1972, they journeyed to Manaus, Brazil. In five years, they lived with jungle humidity and home conditions that most of us would find unbearable. In this atmosphere, they raised up over 25 churches and 3 children.

L. M. learned his Portuguese, took care of his workers and came home only when the call to fill my shoes in administration was made. His diligence in working in the states was no less than that in the Amazon jungle. Whatever the situation, he could be counted on to be steady and firm. If this man made you a promise, you could count on it. He was a constant. Whether living in a hammock on a jungle boat, or leading a church conference, or flying an airplane, L. M. left nothing to chance.

His death was a shock. Flying home to Gainesville, Georgia, one rainy evening, the runway was not where it was expected. L. M. died in the crash. He was the young man I had watched from his youth. I had seen him develop into a strong dedicated leader in Christian service. His death cut short accomplishments that most people never even imagine. When tempted to wonder "what might have been", I am instead filled with gratitude to God for what L. M. was, for the things he did, the quality of character he displayed, and the commitment of his daily life.

*Elmer Moreira
and family*

*Nona Jo, Paco,
and
Ray Alvarado*

The L. M. Reese family

Top down: Louise teaching children of Peru, three generations of men committed to ministry (Allen, Clifford, and Hugh Skelton), Allen & Vicky with the children, Jose Rubio.

EPILOGUE — Through the Eyes of a Son

A "Vision Caster", that's what he is. He's a "man of passion". As a youngster and teen, Allen was like most of us. He did not really appreciate what his father was and could not see the shadow of influence that the man cast. He was the father who was not home; the preacher who was always in a meeting and who seemed to think only of "the work". There was no question of his father's love for him, but there was also no doubt of the importance of the call to minister in the lives of both his parents. So, when he could leave it, he did. The move back to Georgia was a convenient way out of the temptations of easy drugs and fast living just across the border. It was also a move away from a life dominated by church, house guests and constant responsibility to protect the reputation of a missionary family. His version of it all goes like this...

People seemed to forget that I (Allen Skelton) was a part of the family but was not a missionary. I was born to missions, not called of God. At least, not at the age of 18. It would be more than 20 years before I would realize my true destiny.

Like most children growing up, I thought my father was a bit lacking. I never knew him as "father" until I was age 20. There was little relationship, no connecting points. He was always gone, always busy, always immersed in "the work". It wasn't a negative relationship — just a void. I wanted a "cool dad" with lots of money to hand out, status with my buddies, someone about 6 foot 5 and as near a Dallas Cowboy linebacker as he could be. What I had was a gentle, studious father with a zeal toward his calling to be a minister that consumed much of his life. I was loved, and I always respected my parents. My deepest fear was that I would hurt them or their ministry. But, I also wanted to be just exactly like every other kid on the block (or on that short blacktop road in my case.) I was slow to realize what a treasure it was to grow up with the gift of love that never condemned and never berated.

And, as the old story goes, it seems my parents really learned a lot, got a lot wiser, and became much more admirable as I got closer to adulthood. They just got a lot smarter as I grew older. By early 20's, my spiritual rebirth opened my eyes to their world. I began to see in them the things I wanted in my life. Now, by age 46, I find my greatest joy is to travel with Dad, to absorb knowledge from him, to watch him at work and to try to incorporate his insights into my own approach to life.

My father is a man of passion. Few see him as I do but he fits the mold of an "Indiana Jones" to me. This fixer, repairer of things natural and spiritual, this ambassador given to the healing of nations and the calming of strife wherever he goes — he's my father. He has the "cool" of a Clint Eastwood — not the violence or the anger, but a calm unrattled demeanor in all circumstances. Whatever culture or economic strata he enters, he is "at home". All persons receive from him warmth, respect, and a perceptive listening ear. He gives respect, and he receives it. Often, I am awed by the stature he holds in countries that we visit. And yet, he is the same as the quiet man dusting his art objects at home or digging a hole for some new plant he has acquired.

Never have I known a person so fearless in any place and in any circumstance, so knowledgeable of other cultures and other peoples, so courageous to try new things and step out into new territories. Though he is a man of weakness physically, his drive supersedes that weakness and takes him beyond natural ability. He applies himself to constant study. Speaking English and Spanish fluently is not enough. At age 70, he works continually to improve his Portuguese. This is the image that is always before me, an image that calls me to be more than I am.

Having survived those childhood years and the teenage adventures, I finally gave up my tour of occupations to take up my ministry. The years in pastoral ministry were wonderfully fulfilling. Still, I knew inside that my eventual work would be missions — the zeal of my parents burned deep. I just did not know the "when". There was no mention of it, no pushing from my parents. They waited, and I worked at my ministry with a constant glance over my shoulder to see if it was about to get me.

"Allen, I would like to preach for you at a Sunday service." Dad had never asked such a thing.

"No problem. When can you come?" It really was fine, but I knew inside that something special was on the way. This was not like my dad. And, the spirit within me was on edge with the knowledge that this was not "just another sermon."

Dad sat me on the front row of my church some 10 feet away from him as he preached. And, though he preached for the entire congregation in a most remarkable fashion, it was a sermon for me. He preached at me prophetically, something few people really understand. But, for me, the words bore directly into my soul. I had no doubt that he was right on target and that the sermon came not from him but from a much greater source. He did not say words like "You are going to the mission work," but to both of us, that was the clear message. My mind kept saying, "He is saddling you with this calling to missions." My spirit knew he was "passing the torch." My father did not "call" me to church ministry or mission work. I was not pushed in that direction or lectured on the subject during my lifetime. My parents see calling to ministry as a sacred thing to be left to God. But, from my father's anointed lips and in my anointed ears, we both understood the same thing. No longer did I have a choice, and it frightened me. The responsibility to take up the torch and carry it forward weakened me inwardly as nothing before had ever done.

This is the heritage that I carry every day and on every trip. I began with fear. I was following a legend of a minister. How could I ever live up to the standard my father had set? Then, I quit trying to live up to that standard. I learned to walk beside him rather than following him. My ministry is like his and yet very much my own. He makes room for me, and I am constantly alert to learn from him. We laugh together as never before in our lives. I am the constant jokester while he sits quietly grasping every nuance with his wonderful sense of humor.

The unique perspective of life that my parents provide is the priceless heritage of my family. I grew up in and my family lives in the healthiest of atmospheres due to the balance of life my father taught. We are privileged to live on the "cutting edge" of missions. From my wife, Vicky, comes a realistic missions approach and a passion born in her at age 15 when she visited the Missionary Training Center in McAllen and caught the attention of a missionary's kid who was far from spiritual minded. Our three children have all been on numerous missions trips with groups, or with us, or with my parents. We understand that life is for giving. And, our blessings are for sharing. We have been given a unique perspective of life, as have literally thousands of others who have walked with my father at some time on his journey. I call him a "Vision Caster."

Appendix

Church Growth

Though effectiveness of ministry is not measured on charts, the information below indicates the impact of the Rev. Skelton's ministries. From the establishment of his first ministry in Cuba, he has been key to the establishment and growth of the following evangelistic programs in Latin America. (Work with other church organizations and as a trainer of indigenous workers is not included.)

	Work Opened	Churches Year 2000
Cuba	1955	22
Mexico	1963	230
Costa Rica	1966	30
Honduras	1967	360
Brazil	1974	18
Guatemala	1974	36
Nicaragua	1988	28
El Salvador	1988	6
Panama	1994	14
Chile	1998	28

*These ministries all operate under the leadership of citizens from within the countries with the full autonomy of any conference within the Congregational Holiness Church.

BOY SCOUTS OF AMERICA

Notes from various letters

" It will be an honor to welcome you into the ranks of America's outstanding young leaders of tomorrow."

~~ Rance Osborne, 12/22/47

"People will now expect more of you because of this accomplishment {achieving rank of Eagle Scout}. You have worked hard and your standard has been high." ~~ Elbert K. Fretwell, 11/17/47

(National Chief Scout Executive)

"I wish every man in scouting ... could have heard the speech that you made.... Seldom have I heard a grown man speak with the ease and with the fluency that you spoke."

~~ J. B. Loudermilk, 1/9/48

"I was delighted and highly impressed with the talk that you gave. I think it was the best talk of the conference."

~~ J. M. Molder, 1/12/48

"Your talk was outstanding ... As long a America raises such sons as yourself she will always remain the land of the free and the home of the brave."

~~ Charles Bethea, 12/11/49

A Tribute to My Father
~~ *Allen Skelton*

Some things need to be said, while others are best left unsaid.
This is one of those times something should be said.

Basically I am amazed. It has been quite a school watching
you these last two weeks.
Your determination is really something to behold.
It has always been easy to admire you,
but you have raised the stakes.
Your sense of duty is a real motivator to me and others.

They tell us you are a man and you have
a lot of physical problems.
Actually, you are a better definition of a man.
What you endure purely for others
is a quality most men do not have.
The thing that sticks out most of all is that I am impressed.

You are definitely a role model for missions
and Christian ministries.
You have once again made me proud.
I sure have enjoyed our tour of duty together.
I look forward to other times,
but it won't hurt my feelings if you stay good and healthy.

FOR YOUR 25TH WEDDING ANNIVERSARY

In the beginning before they knew there would be love, there was a relationship in the making which God had ordained. While there were yet no thoughts in their hearts of spending eternity together, the preparation for these two to became "one" had already begun. Unbeknown to them, the love they would have would be tried again and again as their never-ending schedule took them to the four corners of the earth. While there was still only a fluttering of their hearts and an occasional touch of their hands, there were plans underway to allow such a depth of love for one another that not even the greatest of hardships or the darkest of powers could sever them.

In the course of time each one began to notice that theirs was more than a surface relationship. They eventually admitted that they were without a doubt in love. However, the Master Planner had in mind to begin to prune them in the very beginning stages of their love. He therefore chose to separate them by distance to see if what had been building was built on a strong foundation. This first real test was to be the first in a series in which they would prove to each other over and over again that their early dream of a life together would be fulfilled by their genuine love and persistent determination to please the other.

With high hopes and a long road ahead of them they legally vowed allegiance to each other nine days into August, 1952. Soon after the honeymoon season came to a close they began preparing for the events they knew would come and started praying about those which they knew nothing of. One of the events they knew nothing of was reminiscing about the first quarter century of their marriage. Few lives could parallel the experiences which they encountered while traveling down the special road they traveled.

At the onset of a brand new life, they made it top priority to find out what God has on His schedule for them. Very few people in this world make any effort at all to come to grips with a force which might have you lay down the common family and social goals to a life of faith.

From this desire to serve, stemmed a story of two super human beings who have touched the lives of countless numbers of people. One of those touched by their lives is one who gives credit of life itself to their existence. Being their son has afforded me first hand knowledge of their lives and activities. This is why on this very special occasion I would like to say I'm proud to be a part of the lives of these beautiful people.

You see I have been there when they gave to those who needed without thought of any favors returned. I've seen how they have given their time, money, clothes and of themselves when there was really no time to give, no money in the bank, no extra clothes to hand out and so tired they could have often paid the price of over extending themselves. These things coupled with the fact of their willingness to perform these acts of kindness only further proved they were genuinely interested and truly loved the people of the world. How many people actually give their lives as servants to God and man without expecting anything in return for their labor?

Truly we who know them can say with an honest heart that we have been blessed by their acquaintance. I can say personally that my life has been and always will be in debt to the priceless raising I received from them. I have received invaluable counseling and guidance to help me better deal with the world in which we live.

These traits mentioned only dust the surface compared to actually what lies inside their hearts. My prayer is that in the next quarter century their lives will continue to be the pillars of faith and the lights for Christ which they have been in the first. With all respect we say, "WE LOVE YOU."

~~ *Allen and Vicky Skelton*

The Cover

Mexican fishermen dip their traditional butterfly nets into the waters of Lake Patzcuaro seeking a harvest of the small white fish so abundant there. Most of them live on the tiny island of Janitzio, a village of small winding streets that reach ever upward to the two dominating fixtures of the island — the Catholic Church and a statue of Benito Juarez.

Until 1964, the religious life of the island was controlled by the church and its prohibition against Protestant missionaries and/or Bibles for the people. It was just such a challenge that Hugh Skelton could not resist. In a "tourist" trip, he emptied his camera gear, filled his camera bag with New Testaments and set out to find a willing recipient. Sitting in a tiny café, he casually commented to the waiter, "I suppose you are a catholic." The reply was negative. The young man had spent time in the United States as a field worker and had been converted to the Pentecostal faith. He was more than pleased to receive and distribute the Testaments.

From that first foray, religious change and tolerance began its inroads. A Protestant church was founded on the island, and two young men were trained for ministry in the Bible School operated in Morelia, Michoacan. Later visits to the island by the Rev. Skelton were for worship in the services regularly held on Janitzio.

Information or additional copies of
this book are available through:

VISION CASTER
3774 Trenton Court, SW
Gainesville, GA 30504

OR

Servant7@bellsouth.net